T0279307

SEEDTIME

THE
SEAGULL
LIBRARY OF
FRENCH
LITERATURE

Philippe Jaccottet

SEEDTIME

NOTEBOOKS

1954–1979

Translated by Tess Lewis

LONDON NEW YORK CALCUTTA

swiss arts council

pr⊃helvetia

This publication has been supported by a grant from
Pro Helvetia, Swiss Arts Council

Seagull Books, 2024

First published in French as Philippe Jaccottet,
Le Semaison: *Carnets, 1954–1979*

© Editions Gallimard, Paris, 1984

First published in English translation by Seagull Books, 2013

English translation © Tess Lewis, 2013

ISBN   978 1 8030 9 359 8

British Library Cataloguing-in-Publication Data

A catalogue record for this book is available from the British Library

Typeset by Seagull Books, Calcutta, India
Printed and bound by WordsWorth India, New Delhi, India

Semaison: The natural dispersion of a plant's seeds.

Littré

1954

May

Attachment to the self renders life more opaque. One moment of complete forgetting and all the screens, one behind the other, become transparent so that you can perceive clarity to its very depths, as far as the eye can see; and at the same time everything becomes weightless. Thus does the soul truly become a bird.

1955

January

Snow covers the fine grass. It whirls as it falls like the seeds of maples and settles like a single vast and silent seed onto the village.

Or the sliver of moon above black twigs.

1956

September

Just as the moon is the sun's mirror, water is light that
sinks into the earth, a cool light, a September sky.
A star is a flame of water, a frozen fire.
Everything turns blue like a face shadowed by desire or
sorrow under tousled hair.
Everything turns blue, especially the distant mountains.
Nearer to us, we can still discern boulders and trees of a
lighter colour than the others.
There is a sense of a tender lull.

October

The reeds: how their velvety ears burst, letting loose a slow stream of seeds, an entire crop, in complete *silence*.
Human birth: cries of pain, blood.
In absolute silence, the plant rends with a soft, irresistible languor and disperses its seeds, trusting them to the wind.

1958

January

Columns of snow are blown across fields, roads and
    hills,
truncated or twisted by the wind,
frail, fearful stars,
restless constellations of crystal
that a puff of wind could transform into tears.
Thrown to ground, these routed armies
are now but a trickle.
Throughout the night, the wind growled like flames in
    an oven.
At dawn, the snow was still in flight under low clouds
    and a sun, only slightly higher, was visible through
    its sheets.

May. MAJORCA

Almond groves in the evening, their trunks black. Towering palm bushes like piles of green fans. Pine forests and, beyond them, dark mountains. Or else the blue of the sea between the trunks and the greenery, but the word blue doesn't capture it. It's too gentle. Black would almost be preferable but it too would be wrong. An accumulation of blue, dense and thick, like a wall. In any case, not an opening. A wealth of blue. Nothing moves or glitters. No patches of colour either. Intense, but calm, motionless, opaque, unfathomable. A blue presence, as strong as the earth, as heavy and as rich, but indivisible, without details. The entire landscape, as well, as seen from inside a forest, almost immobile though airy, at once strong and light, vibrant and calm, powerful but without ostentation, vertical rather than horizontal.

The plants old, hard, thorny, but not at all sparse as in Provence. A silent and powerful wealth, without cries but also without murmurs. Without the slightest trace of a river or of running water, no springs, and yet not arid. The heat too is powerful and constant but gently fanned by the sea.

An orderly congregation of strong presences, abundant and calm. A powerful serenity. An immense tribunal. An authoritarian display but no voice is strained.

Luminous monuments, vast, airy domains. Without vehemence. Giovanni Gabrieli's brass. Gold, perhaps, but no jewels.

In this season the house is but a reserve of shadows, a small fortress against the sun's armies, a reservoir, a redoubt of freshness. Archers, breastplates, banners surround it. A great clashing of arms resounds over the sea. An image possible at any moment, but which must be overcome, erased.

Wealth, power outside the walls: a constant, immobile force, a calm authority of space, the mechanical sound of the sea. You could almost forget the infinite weightlessness of your burdens.

The sonorous forest.

The rocks. Here and there they resemble pages an enormous hand has pressed tightly into a file, like the pages of a book under a press before they are bound. More often they are scattered in great disorder, carved out by the sea in all directions, perforated, upended, shattered. Between the sea's moving splendour and the ground's calm fecundity.

Plants that resist the wind, that can tremble only with their tips.

The shock of a relentless force against an immovable power, fundamentally, immensely silent: a white fire flares at this borderline, an explosion of water drops, a sudden flowering that withers immediately. Time uses us this way and our works spark briefly under its blows.

November

Trails of fire in the grass before a snowfall
like flares in the western sky before night
the soul's start before death
a warrior who adorns himself with wounds

❧

That furore over the abyss
those sorrows, those smiles, those labours,
the slow construction of monuments, of pavilions,
over the abyss those wars, those wounds,
yes, so much sorrow, violence, passion,
those painstaking calculations, those monstrous
      convoys of arms,
those explosions, the collapsing,
a whirlwind of more or less golden leaves
over the infinite chasm
and yet . . .
      of this battle between the abyss and its prey, how-
      ever doomed the prey or triumphant the abyss,
I still cannot say which will be the victor if there is a
victor, if we can speak of victory,
if this imperious image is not false,
if, in capturing it, my glance has not already

surpassed it, if in saying battle I have not
predicted peace, prepared the way . . .
O secret of battle, visible in the flight of leaves,
visible in the chasm, yet still undeciphered,
O darkness that I grasp in my fist like a torch,
Like a woman's hair and dark falcon in the gloom

❧

Stars veiled by trees, by the mist, winter's face.

December

Just before eight o'clock, under a completely overcast sky, the world is nothing but brown, a table of earth. Here, a lamp shines in the street, yellow like a rayless sun, there a golden door opens, a shadow watches to see what the weather will be in the garden.

ح

From a distance, the mobile, translucid constellations of rain on the windows are only moving veils, curtains closing. The panting, irregular south wind. The mechanical north wind.

1959

January

Ice, transparency, sun. Very few clouds, small, hanging on the mountains. Everything is purified, the ornaments have fallen away, only the essential forms remain. In the morning, the ground in the garden is hard, as if riddled with icy dew, then slightly damp all day. Dream of writing a poem as crystalline and alive as a piece of music, pure enchantment, but not frigid. Regret for not being a musician, for lacking a musician's skill, his liberty. A music of common speech, enhanced here and there with an appoggiatura, perhaps, with a limpid trill, a pure and tranquil delight for the heart with just a touch of melancholy because it is all so fragile. I am ever-more convinced that there is no greater offering one can give, if one has the gift, than such music, heart-rending not because of what it expresses but through its sheer beauty. Nothing is explained, but its perfection surpasses any possible explanation. Jean Racine sometimes, Francesco Petrarch, flashes in Luis de Góngora y Argote, Louise Labé? Arnaud Daniel? Maurice Scève?

እ.

Since the snow or the daisy at the peak of its flowering have been extinguished, all light has fled to the sliver of moon.

୫

Thin moon over brown lands before sunrise.

୫

First snow, which is barely snow since it melts as soon as it nears the ground, but suddenly everything has become gloomy. The wind blows snow everywhere, raising it higher than the roofs. It thickens abruptly then scatters as erratically as a swarm of midges in good weather. The sky is a uniform shade of light grey, except for a slightly brighter hue above the hills.

February

In the morning, hail.

At night, after the snow has fallen continuously, a landscape of white, brown and black seldom seen here. An almost weightless covering on the trees, as if we were looking through gauze. A childlike joy spread through the village: old men threw snowballs.

March

Birds in the rain. Flowering trees in the rain. The air like an enormous window trembling in its frame. The first buds on the chestnut trees. Wallflowers, anemones.

April

Ferocious mistral. Mont Ventoux hidden in a pink-grey
mist.

October

This evening, golden light in the frigid air. How quickly it leaves the trees and rises towards clouds carried away by the wind. In the garden, dead acacia leaves, pale yellow, the first to fall; every day they cover the ground. Those of the Japanese persimmon change with more flair, more gradually, with more nuance as their fruit ripens. Though still green, the peach tree grows lighter. The vine is almost bare, old, sick. Colours of autumn daisies or little chrysanthemums, so well attuned to the season. A bush, pink from top to bottom.

And now gold turns to pink and the green of the fields and trees deepens, turning from yellow-green to blue-green. Arrows of wind. The road is the colour of water, of slate. Some clouds are already like smoke. Intimacy of light in the room, on the white page that has in turn taken on a pink tinge. An envelope of shadows on the books, the objects. Nothing but the sound of wind and words.

Soon night will make it impossible to write without a lamp. Day lasts only in the sky's highest realm. We turn our backs to the sun.

Purple clouds, violet. The paper is almost blue. A dying fire. I can barely see the words.

The other side of the sky is still golden, while blue takes over the east. Silver-gold. Day-night.

Raise the ornament above the night once more, over the abyss. A dreamt-of ornament: at once learned and musical, firm and muted, vast and hidden. Models: Friedrich Hölderlin, Giacomo Leopardi, some poems by Charles Baudelaire.

An effortless movement in the infinite. Birds. Other examples, the most beautiful, perhaps, in Dante: *Dolce color d'oriental zaffiro . . . (gentle hue of oriental sapphire . . .)* But no more Thomism today, no sacred numbers, etc. Solitude, withdrawal, threats, the sapphire is all the sweeter.

Reservations (absurd, of course!) with regard to Leopardi's allegories and thought, tension in Hölderlin, Baudelaire's posing.

Perhaps it is time to try something else, in which lightness and gravity, reality and mystery, detail and space enter into a harmony that is not quiescent but alive. Grass, air. Infinitely fragile and beautiful glimpses —as of a flower, a jewel, gold work—placed in the extraordinary immensity. Stars and night. A vast and fluid discourse, airy, in which jewels of language are discreetly placed. Just as something reappears now and again in the mist. Or else, the way you suddenly remember the depths of space and time while busy with some menial task.

November

Naive questions. Why is this beautiful, but not that? Direct experience that occurs frequently in your work: this is dishonest and that is not, or is less dishonest. An order, therefore, a hope?

Leopardi maintains that beauty is an illusion and therefore a trap. But how is it that beauty exists, that he surrendered to its power, that he served it so well? How can you deny that beauty expresses something essential, how can you reduce it to a simple lie? Must we be so wary of it? Even if everything thwarts us and uses us, directly or indirectly?

෨

It is not certain that modern times, for all its negative aspects—an enormous mass that blocks the sky—does not also have a happy message for us: that we are children of time and that everything is given to us through time, that opposites cannot be dissolved and that we are neither able nor allowed to rise above contradictions; that we must simply prevent one term from dominating the other.

Our condition is very strange because it does not allow for substantial progress, because we have never got close to a definitive answer. We know we will not arrive at an answer and yet we keep asking because the urge to question is an essential part of our nature. What is strange is that no experience, whether religious or philosophical, can be had for others. It must be experienced afresh, relived each time in order to be valid. We must always start again.

Hence the irritating feeling of treading water: *seinesgleichen geschieht (experience repeats itself)*, says Robert Musil.

The same is true for the inspiration that is the source of many poems. Someone says more or less, 'I had the impression that the order of the world had been revealed to me,' or else 'I understood the language of the birds,' or 'The veil that usually separates us from the real was torn away.' (This is also a theme in fairy tales.) Obviously, the subject here is an experience, an undeniable *fact* (you can dismiss it as mendacious, but it occurs none-theless); this experience can take various forms, but the result is always the same. It has happened since the beginning of mankind and hundreds of examples can be found in mystical, philosophical or purely literary texts. One could object that such an experience is a *mirage*: But how is this mirage possible, and why shouldn't it, even as a mirage, be meaningful?

This mirage, or this intuition, revelation or dream, opposes order against disorder, fullness against the void, and wonder, hope and enthusiasm against disgust. Is it possible to believe that the human obsession with order in the most diverse realms is utterly meaningless? And do we not have the duty, or at least the right, to listen to this profound, irresistible nostalgia, as if it had something important and true to tell us? Isn't the refusal to believe in an enigma that attracts and enlightens us the act of a blinkered spirit? Is believing solely in bones, in ruin, more justified? If we became more flexible, wouldn't we, in fact, feel a rush of life? Let us remain true to our immediate experience rather than turning our attention to whatever may contradict it externally.

ક્ર

To advance from uncertainty, nonetheless. Owning nothing, because aren't all acquisitions paralysing? Uncertainty is the motor, the shadow is the source. I walk for lack of a place, I talk because I don't know— proof that I'm not dead yet. Stammering, I'm not yet thrown to ground. All that I've done serves no purpose, even if it is admired or considered an accomplishment. *Magician of insecurity, the poet* . . . , René Char spoke truly. I breathe because I still know nothing. *Moving, horrible, exquisite earth*, Char also said. Explain nothing, but say it true.

Yet how to begin again? There's the rub. By what twisted, indirect path? By what absence of paths? Starting from destitution, weakness, doubt. Forgetting the past helps, as does contempt for what has been accomplished and praised, advised or suggested to writers today.

Above all in defiance of the levelling of souls. Not the cast-offs of knights and princes, but their pride, their reserve. There is no poetry without superiority. Of this, at least, I am certain and this certainty gives me strength in the absence of another strength. But no castles: streets, rooms, paths, our life.

છે

Simone Weil: *That is why, whenever we truly give our attention, we destroy some evil within us.* Later: *Attention consists in suspending thought, in leaving it free, open and accessible to the object, it consists in holding the diverse knowledge we have acquired and must make use of near our thought, but at a level inferior to it and not in contact with it.* Later: *One should not seek out the most precious gifts, but wait for them.*[1]

છે

Autumn, rainy fire, old fire, pyre. Scrap iron, wood and mist. Rust, cinders. Ashy dawn, consumed, the celebration ended, decorations torn, faded. Armed mists, marching over fields and gardens. The ploughshare of the cold advances and glistens. Standing behind it, the shadow ploughs.

. . . And yet, I have seen the fields, the trees and narrow valleys again as they always were in this season when a beautiful day interrupts a stretch of rainy or windy weather. I rediscovered autumn's weak light on the oak trees' trunks and the kind of golden hum under leaves held up on strong arms or trunks like black columns; the yellow poplars too, motionless along a body of unseen water; and the curves of the earth that almost nothing obscures; and tables of rock among low trees, thorny bushes mixing dark green with rust red; and the glittering furrows; some pigeons take flight with the sound of applause or washing snapping in the wind and two of them, whiter than the others, inscribe the pure line of their flight into the blue of the sky. Then, as soon as the clouds on the horizon veil the sun, everything turns almost dark and the cold sweeps over the landscape like a scythe. Smoke rises here and there.

Speak with this emptiness in your heart, speak against it. Acacia sprigs against the almost blue white of the sky. Burning dead leaves, pulling out weeds—perhaps restrict yourself to this.

These shoots with their last leaves, thin and pale. Winter setting in.

❧

Columns of rain on the march, rain in ruins
all is ruin including he who speaks of ruin
but he desperately fights against it however he can
or delays it or snatches from it a few rays of light.

꒰꒱

Fed on shadows, I speak
and chewing over the meagre crop of darkness
poor, weak, leaning against the ruins of the rain
I find support in what I cannot doubt—
doubt—and, inhabiting the uninhabitable, I look
and again I start muttering against death
at death's dictation. In collapsing I persist
in seeing, I see the ruin that shines,
the entire distance of the earth,
and, vaguely illuminated, the very depths of the age,
an unbearable gentleness,
a wing under a dark cover of clouds.
Shadows open my eyes,
and neither the approach of the impossible in the
    depths of the day
nor the invasion of ash into my core silences me.
Victorious, insolent, fierce, they dictate
new phrases as a last resort,
and I grope among the ancient words,
among the ruins of ancient verses,
but Ah! with no other support or guidance
than the force of error,
a silent obscurity that carries no lamp.

꒰꒱

Just as after too long a story, when nothing remains
    but broken columns and rats' nests among the
    banners,
must we really despair?
Aren't these so many lies that have been made fragile
    again?
I will lean back on the column of rain
to celebrate the wind's triumph.

※

Still supported by the interminable dark
and pushed from behind by brutal night
at the end of my strength in this November dawn
I see the cold's plough advance, blazing,
and behind it, in a brighter light,
darkness tills.

※

I speak for this shadow that departs at the end of the day
or is it, rather, that the shadow sings as it goes,
its footsteps speaking, as it covers the fields,
with all the gentleness of distance?
What is this air more melodious than air,
if not the very act of rending and the earth's distance
that murmurs lovingly, if not the hours
that form a chain of words as they pass?

Those who disappear do not weep, but sing.
Trees, houses, flowers all fade one by one
down to the paths darkness treads with a steady pace,
with half-closed eyes fixed on the source.
And there where the darkness finally slips out of sight,
the breath of a mountain rises,
so docile and hidden, barely higher than the dark.

≈

Into your hand that will no longer touch
the earth's roughness or smoothness, I slip this leaf,
not quite a wing, nor quite a bright arrow
to serve as a guide, or a lamp, or an offering;
against the voracity of the abyss
it has only the power of the invisible. What it says
can do no more than defy ruin's thunder
with what can neither be seen, nor believed, nor
    asserted
directly or through images. And yet it is this
I give you. What the leaf brings is like a faint trace in
    the snow
of a passage that proves there is no smile but fades,
and no smile is born but under
time's hatchet.

≈

How will you remain upright in this devastation
   of worlds
collapse, storm, invasion of infinities
whose triumph, flanked by rows of the vanquished,
advances amidst our ruins carrying trophies of stars.
None of our dreams will remain intact
nor will our refuges.
Where will you find footing, and where your heart
nourishment? The world slides, the seasons
slip away, and the purest lines are blurred.
The worlds' connections are severed, some disintegrate,
some move apart, but depth
and distance can no longer be grasped.

Will there be any tears pure enough
to clear a path for us through these lands?
But what if it's no longer a question of lands, of paths,
of nights to get through, if there is no longer any
land or day or expanse?
If the source of tears has dried up?
If the wind, no, not just the wind, if the storm,
or rather the storm within storms,
carries away the slightest statements
along with the mouth that spoke them and the faces
that bent towards its gentleness, and this gentleness
   in turn
carries off this outburst
like a fire turning in on itself
and consuming the memory of fire, the name of fire,

even the possibility of fire,
if the sea withdraws from the sea, and if the worlds,
all the worlds, roll up like a tent at the breaking of camp?
Who can still speak if there is no air?
None before us would have dreamt up blinder
     fantasies
Nor had a closer view of a greater disorder.

ન્ડ

I see the sign of gold on the linden tree.
Like the sacrifice, in the *Odyssey*, of a cow with gilded
     horns.
That which grips us as it consumes itself, disappears.
     Burning wood. In me, through my lips, only death
     has spoken. All poetry is the voice given to death.
     May our decay praise, celebrate. May our defeat
     shine, resound.
If I were not approaching the end, I would not see.
Birds circling or shooting like arrows across the sky,
     no one sees you but the dying, those who are being
     worn down, who are slowly turning to dust.
Vision and voice of the destroyed.

ન્ડ

Vast winter landscape. La Tuilière.
The slope on the left is entirely covered with oaks:
     holm oaks in dark, dusty green, oaks with withered
     leaves, just like dirt.

Two herds: one white, one light brown.

The meadows' borders in greyish green. Paths.

Below, the River Lez beneath bare trees with trunks
mostly straight and slender, their delicate clusters
are surprising and difficult to describe—like
smoke? Something weightless that rises and
branches out, light coloured, almost pink. The
word *smoke* is too grey, too soft.

In the distance, Mont Ventoux with its gleaming,
snow-covered dome.

A few farms painted with the sharp light.

Stones, ploughed fields. Faded remains of flowers.

1960

February

'Someone will place a seed in your hand
so that even once your hand has been destroyed
nothing will have been taken from you or broken.'

Words said without knowing the rest,
to accompany you in doubt and suffering,
folly's trust in the unknown.

Still, these words are imprecise or false
because there has been no gift, no seed
no destruction, nothing that will break,

Because it's a matter of defying the grave
of tearing down reason and human appearance
like prisons too narrow and precise.

Words ventured in order to be more brave
To make your bearing more grave
And to clear a way for such a seed.

᪥

Wood differs from earth only in form. Everything here is the colour of earth, almost pinkish, up to where snow has pitched its camp. I contrast a fire of old wood with the snow, with the snowy buds of the almond tree. Spring's overture. A few words scattered here and there, ethereal.

This is the time to mention a vast expanse of air, of movement, of splendour, of animation, above the solid, the ancient, the immemorial, barely decorated with garlands of flowers, crowned with laurels. A land exposed, while elsewhere in winter the snow hides the ground and softens all forms. There are few places where the earth is more visible: the ground, the foundation. But the rock is not heavy: it is serious, severe. It reminds one of invincible warriors, though without arrogance or flamboyance, with a true and silent power that permits and purifies the joyful animation in the air above.

Almond and peach blossoms, compared to those of cherry, apple and plum, the pride of the north. There is an excess, almost ostentation, to those foamy spheres above the high grasses, themselves in bloom. But here, these flowers are the epitome of delicacy in the still cool air on naked branches above the bare earth—both branches and earth almost the same colour—and this combination of the rough and the refined, much like an alliance between old age and frail youthfulness, is one of the wonders of the world. Show it, grasp it: dust and flower, wood and silk. What is there to say about this white, this pink? The pink of flesh is of another order and the word 'rose' has too many associations that would have to be eliminated here, especially the erotic overtones.

Because we are concerned here with what is most pure.

So that even the trees' wounds do not seem as repulsive, as frightening as human or animal wounds. Strange. Where does the horrible begin? Wood and leaves don't repulse or horrify. Horror of blood. A stream of sap is just a tear. That's why comparisons of the human and the vegetal are doubtful, despite a thousand traditional metaphors. Novalis: *Infinite remoteness from the world of flowers.*

The first wallflowers, drops of yellow at the bottom of dark-green chalices.

How the catkins open, this fur out of which silently bursts a long-lasting firework display, a nebula almost, or powder. This happens without the slightest discernible sound—yet another source of astonishment. Their entire life is expressed in colours, forms, movements.

The first birdsongs, like a bubbling in the trees overhead.

❧

The mountain always appeared with traces of snow on its peak above the Rebavas road, like something Greek, a snowy owl's nest, a thin banner or Tibetan prayer

31

flags. A place high in the thin air, a white bird above bare trees.

Or the elbow of the distant river at the base of the barely green slope: you see a watery shade of light green—there are semi-precious stones of this colour (jade, opals?)—and one or two vivid lines of foam slanting across it to show its seemingly stationary rapid movement—surging waters of late winter—and on the banks the bare trees, their smooth trunks of a grey turned slightly yellow or pink in the weak light and their branches reaching upwards and straight, unlike the twisted, knotty trees that live amidst the rocks. A place of fragile ascension, a fog of branches, so different from the clusters, the portentous circles of oaks covered with ivy, with their black force, their chains, their heavy grilles retaining or defending some unknown austerity, some upturned stone, well or tomb. Circles, solemn, grave assemblies round a silence—and the hoopoes or sultana birds live in the branches, places to stay, to wait, motionless, with a sovereign resolve; while all along the river, everything is in motion, water, smoke, a lane under the light arch of vapours, a shining road.

Like two lives, two possible ways of thinking: one knotty, attentive, reflective and tied to the night, to stone, druidic, bent over the mouth of the earth; the other lively, light, almost insolent or nimble, along the glittering thread of days.

Almond trees, foam, snows, peaks of coolness, luminous plumage, swans . . .

❧

Days mild from the earliest morning hours, luminous, with the first movements of birds.

March

Enter the circle of oaks.

Chains hung with ivy.

Take shelter in their severity, the light is tempered by
their leaves.

Silence, rest, anticipation.

At least once, we will have been in this place.

Then everything explodes; not only is this place gone,
but even the memory, the celebration of this place.
Torn garlands, broken columns, twisted chains, but
that, still, is not much: the ground, the table cracks.
There will only have been one flash in the enclosure
of wood and leaves. Scattered hoopoe feathers. The
birth of a star. Our thought nonetheless can grasp
this. Thought will also be dispersed, sparse words,
even the most pure.

Enter the assembly of sombre oaks crowned with gold
and imagine their destruction.

Pass under arches of mist
in the fog of the riverside trees
follow the sign of foam on jade
the colour of swollen rivers in late winter.

The earth on both sides of this passage is fed with
    water
and wears a precocious green. A breeze rises,
a fresh breeze passes.
rays are thrown from the mirror of ice to the mirror of
    the sea
according to the ground's incline.
An easy flow, glittering from one end to the other,
especially where the rocks oppose it.
Another of the world's lessons.

෨

Speak also of the flower that rests on the wood, on the
dust; and the rock garland with ivy, monument or
ancient tomb, decorated with this green bronze, like
some kind of warrior's laurel crown. Old things, mas-
sive, strong, dark, *tenacious*, noble, silent, immobile.
Maybe the dripping of a wellspring at its base and a
primrose offering, springtime honey, a tiny cup or snow-
drop, a milky bell.

Ancient tomb or monument,
Ornamented only with tenacious ivy,
a garland evoking in those who walk past
the bronze of war or night's greenery.
At its base, offered up from some intimate source
to those who draw near as to those who depart
a bowl of honey, a milky bell.

Or:

Massive urn or ancient shrine
unadorned but for tenacious ivy,
a garland reminding those passing by
of the bronze of war or the leaves' nocturnal shine.

The primrose offers its honey-filled bowl
And the snowdrop its milky bell
To the one commemorated here
And to the living who draw near.

೭෴

In the evening, the dark's great wing spreads over the
fields, the gardens, while in the distance Mont Ventoux
still shines intact.

Towards the base, the foundation grows darker,
more green, made more poignant by an obscure mem-
ory of childhood, by time that has collected in the
grasses. The distant summit grows pinker, more golden,
more luminous. Wisps of smoke blow quickly over a
garden. But there are flowers in the sky, shreds of fire,
light moulded into clouds. The highest elevations shine
brightest.

Orion seems to want to tip westwards.

The night, cloudy, dark, without depth, with flat or twisted shapes, whitish slopes, as if someone were holding a lamp behind the clouds at various points in the sky, more to frighten than to illuminate and guide. The damp curtains in a theatre where nothing good will happen. Pallor. Above the familiar landscape, known almost by heart, this space suddenly seems strange, an El Greco sky. And yet, there is only a bit of mist behind which the ornate geography lies intact, knots tied by the wind, the agitated breath of forests and the earth in springtime, damp rags.

Peach tree blossoms: an impression of crowds, of throngs, of droning in the budding which has always struck me as the clearest sign of early spring. A silent explosion, too. But the multiplicity, the multitude is most striking. And then the first flower opens in the rain, like a pink star. Constellation of the peach tree. It is the colour of dawn. Peach tree, constellation of dawn.

Contemplating the earthly zodiac, a galaxy trapped in a garden. Soon it will be the acacia's turn, I haven't forgotten it and I would not have believed it could be so lavish. Scents, whiteness, night in May or June, the shortest of the year.

Fields of wheat, mirrors lined with wrinkles, waves, shudders. The spirit races over these lands without stopping.

Slanting rain, changeable, passing or fleeing; the sound of a machine, indeterminate, perhaps in the fields. Days still almost frigid, malevolent. The sound of cars is also that of a machine, a tool that would delve into the substance of air in order to pierce it.

Brief words like quick rain. Like the lines it leaves for an instant on the window, shining, starlit, and yet each pearl, each drop has its own knot of shadow. Behind the star of tears, the grass is somewhat greener, a similar multitude in the nest of trees. Blue smoke like distance.

෨෴

Come near again, Destroyer,
That I may look upon your face and it give me counsel
    in shattering.
But it is I who approach and I believe I see him before me
Behind the mask scented with carnival violets
Isn't it urgent to know him before he breaks my
    bones?
But he takes the question out of my mouth,
he disarms me, scattering me like almond flower petals
and the more I search, the more he misleads me,
the more I want to defy him, the larger he grows and
    escapes me.
I've already given up earthly concerns to contemplate
    only him
when he attacks beauty, when he demolishes the
    city walls.

In him I saw the source of day,
and in him I must also learn to recognize
the one who poisons the waters.
I must contain in one invisible reality
Both source and ashes, lips and a dead rat's carcase.
I was too quick to praise him for what daylight he
    spreads,
his revenge is to seem unspeakable in this clarity,
refusing me peace at so low a price,
regaining vigour in this exquisite guise.

❧

A gentleness like that of light
when the sun's rays, as it sets in the west, are longer
    and more golden,
a breath of gentleness imparted to things nearby
out of compassion for their coming demise,
a gentleness that defies the enemy's crudeness
a firm patience in the face of torturing time,
the gift of gentleness inexhaustibly condemned on all
    sides
by an inexhaustible response.

❧

Past noon, the light is bruised,
it admits it is muddied and its only task now
is to impose order on its own collapse.

It is the Completely Other that we try to grasp. How to explain that we search for it and never find it, yet keep searching? The infinite is the *breath* that animates us. The unknown is a breath; God is a breath. We cannot grasp him. Poetry is the word this breath feeds and carries, hence its power over us.

All poetic activity is devoted to reconciling, or at least bringing together, the finite and the infinite, clarity and obscurity, breath and form. That is why the poem returns us to our centre, to our central concern, to a metaphysical question. The breath pushes, rises, expands, disappears; it animates and eludes us; we try to grasp it without stifling it. And so we invent a language that combines rigour and vagueness, in which measure does not hinder movement but shows it and therefore keeps it from dissipating completely.

It is possible that beauty is born when the finite and the infinite become visible at the same time, that is to say, when we see forms but recognize that they do not express everything, that they do not stand only for themselves, that they leave room for the intangible. There is no beauty, at least for our eyes, in the purely intangible, nor is there beauty in forms without depth, forms completely expressed and unfolded. But there is no limit to the possible combinations of the finite with the infinite, and this is the source of art's variety. In Rembrandt, the finite is a powerful presence. In Ingres, there is almost nothing but forms, and, despite his accomplished technique, his painting is weak. In Chardin and in Braque, one could say the infinite has been tamed, subdued, like fire in a lantern. Still, that cannot be the *whole* of art either. In the *Divine Comedy*, the infinite is what imposes form upon the finite; everything is ordered within a grandiose structure justified by a truly great vision. It takes prodigious intellectual effort to give form to the Absolute.

Even if man continues to push back his limits, the infinite will not become smaller; otherwise it would not be infinite. Therein lies the mistake made by certain moderns who conceive of the infinite in quantitative terms and who believe that man makes gains on the infinite if he successfully starts to stride across the heavens. But the sky has been a symbol of the infinite only as long as the sky itself appeared infinite, inaccessible. Now, nothing visible seems beyond man's reach. Yet the truly invisible has not changed, diminished or weakened in the slightest; it has simply found its true nature, which is without images. Now God is truly spirit, and absolutely beyond the reach of images, except negative ones. God cannot even be called God any more. He will no longer be taken for a king.

This is no reason to believe that there are no longer any forms, or limits or visible, finite things. But we must be more attentive to the way we use words. We should, in truth, be asking ourselves if God had ever been more powerful than today, since His death has been proclaimed.

≥&

Strange, all this.

I've contemplated the face of night and the jewels with which it adorns its remoteness. Elusive sultana, the lower part of her face hidden behind a veil of lunar mist, seared, charred beauty, an ember no hand can grasp.

≥&

Outside, inside: What do we mean by inside? Where does outside end? Where does inside begin? The white page belongs to the outside, but the words written on it? All of the white page is in the white page, and therefore outside of me, but all of the word is not contained in the word. That is to say that there is a sign I write down as well as its meaning; at first the word is in me, then it leaves me and, once written, looks like tracery, like a design in the sand; but it keeps something hidden, something perceived only by thought. Thought is the inside, and the outside is everything thought seizes on, all that affects and touches it. Thought itself has no form, weight or colour; but it uses forms, weights and colours, it plays with them according to certain rules. All that is surprising. The heart is not the inside; in fact the true *inside* cannot be subjected to such localization. There are organs in us and these organs have an inside, but one can go no further: that inside is still outside, visible to a certain extent, something with form, weight colour.

But the inside that we set against the outside (when, for example, we speak of the inner life) is not at all inside or outside, or rather only inside in a certain sense. Like radio waves emitted and received, it circulates and materializes when it comes into contact with the outside. *Deus interior intimo meo*, God deeper within me than myself, absolutely inside, absolutely not outside. God, the inside of the word. Breath. Those who wield words are closer to God. It is their duty to respect the word because it conveys breath instead of hiding, fixing, extinguishing it. The word is a passage, an opening for the breath. For this reason we like valleys, rivers, roads, air. They direct us towards the breath. Nothing is finished. One must sense that exhalation and sense that the world is but a passing shape of breath.

Perhaps rhythmic speech is a more or less fortunate imitation of that breath. It conveys a sense of expansion, of rising that nonetheless submits to a certain order, a form, and is therefore neither dissipated nor wasted. Everything is a provisional suspension of breath, a moment's rest for the perpetually breathing divinity. The entire universe is like a breath suspended. Just as when the wind dies in the garden, then picks up again and things change. But nothing is lost. Divinity breathes eternally.

The invisible power, the heart of the world breathes again for a moment: trees and mountains are born; but an attentive eye will note their precariousness, their movement, their transitory, uncertain nature.

੨੦

The finite should not be stronger than the infinite: this is our era's misfortune. Poetics that are harmful to poetry or, at least, dangerous to it. We know all too well what we should do. And yet we must still follow that which is our own truth and keeps us from imitating the old masters. Everything begins again from constraints and uncertainties, from new difficulties. There too is hope: in obscurity, in impossibility. One cannot deny this starting point, which nonetheless seems like a trap from which there is no escape.

੨੦

Cioran: *Yet, does a void that offers plenitude, a fulfilling void—does it not contain more reality than all history possess from beginning to end?*[2]

੨੦

Meister Eckhart: . . . *I shall again say what I have never said before. God and Godhead are as far apart from each other as heaven and earth. I say further: the inner and the outer self are as far apart as heaven and earth. But with God the distance is many thousands of miles greater. That is, God* becomes *and* unbecomes . . .

Later:

When I was still in the ground, in the depths, in the flood and source of the Godhead, no one asked me where I wished to go or what I was doing. But as I flowed forth, all creatures uttered: 'God.' If someone were to ask me: 'Brother Eckhart, when did you leave your house?', then I was in there. This is how all creatures speak of God. And why do they not speak of the Godhead? All that is in the Godhead is One, and of this no one can speak. God acts, while the Godhead does not act . . .

[W]hen I enter the ground, the bottom, the flood and the source of the Godhead, no one asks me where I come from or where I have been. There no one has missed me . . .

Whoever has understood this sermon, I wish them well. Had no one been here, I would still have had to preach it to this collecting-box.[3]

Musil read such words as promises.

❧

Góngora, *First Solitude*, v. 940–9 (at the end of the ball, the fiancée goes to assist the games):

[L]ike a new phoenix dressed in plumes as brilliant as rays of the morning sun, accompanied
  by the lyric monarchy

that cuts through air and, fording clouds, crowns with foam
  the king of all the rivers:
on its banks now the wind inherits trophies
  deserted and not small
  of barbarous funeral rites
erected by Egypt for her Ptolemies.

This marvellous taste for expanding space and decorating it with absent or distant trophies. And the extreme density of expression:

Pequeños no vacios

And the fireworks, v. 1066–1071:

Solicitous Juno, attentive Love . . .
lead the couple to their house
crowned by fixed and falling stars
that resolve in sounding smoke.[4]

Góngora's language, like that of St John of the Cross, could be described with exactly the same words as the landscape of Majorca: air, gold, rock.

❧

At the end of winter, who shows us the way?
Through the forest, the sickle of snow.

❧

How childish it is to imagine a cruel god! If God exists, he can be neither good nor bad. What then is this weakness, this malfunction in a machine otherwise admirable in so many ways? Could our difficulty in understanding evil perhaps signify that we have *misconceived* it, that, when faced with this problem, our thinking is faulty or has reached a limit?

Can nothing veil Fate's dreadful injustice?

èa

The poem in long, regular lines no doubt presupposes a relatively deep and peaceful breath, an equilibrium I have lost or that I can no longer maintain naturally and continuously. Everything made solemn, instants, agreement, harmony, happiness. But how do you progress from certain poetic notations to a poem? The voice dies away too quickly. There is an interesting problem in the opposition of the 'poem as instant' (such as Giuseppe Ungaretti's *Allegria*) to the 'poem as discourse' that has always been mine, like a faintly solemn story, chanted a few inches above the earth.

How can you convey a sense of this fragile equilibrium or make it permanent, like a column of glass or even of water supported by the void? We are supported by the poem itself and it is a frail support, somewhat deceptive. It gleams and collapses: a waterfall heard in the night. Confusion of the poem and its object.

Beautiful days.

This morning, the snow on Mont Ventoux gleams in two spots, very low, on the eastern ridge. Foliage glistens like water in the large green patch of the 'château's' meadow. These greens, a bit yellowed and so fresh, of the new leaves. Such beauty seems a challenge or an insult to the heart: the human is so inadequate before this order.

In February, I saw the light plunge its brilliant shaft into this same meadow of vibrant green.

The conifers are dark, immutable columns in this landscape where the oaks are still just a pink haze, a bit more than haze surely: like a layer of earth that is much lighter, less dense than real earth, a haze, but a haze of earth held up by branches, exalted by the trunks; banners, fans, crowns or corollas of pink earth, suspended earth pinker for being suspended, through which we can make out garlands, chains, twists of ivy. While the chestnuts are already an unfathomable abundance of leaves, and the linden and acacia trees are just budding, each species offering another number, another complement of leaves, another nuance. Between noon and four, however, the light is too even, too dull and the tableau frozen.

Beautiful backlight. The walls appear black and the early wheat and new grass are intensely luminous, as if illuminated from within by gold, the yellow of gold. The ploughed fields are black, too. This is the section of the landscape that lies to the west, near the cemetery, the chapel and the ancient marshland—it is a rather large valley, mild, more damp. The Rochecourbière plateau with its oaks and boulders begins at the valley's edge; and over this plateau is air, a fever of space, a flight.

≈

The wing lifted, turned, was gilded.
Gold on its tip and over it, deep shadows.
It is the hour when air takes flight, when the ground
    blazes,
When the highest air freezes . . .

≈

White and green pear trees, white and yellow-green cherry trees. The scenery of the western Eautagnes, the blonde willows, the shades of green, its landscape gardens, its golden peaks in the evening.

Still spring: the mixture of cold and heat. Warm gusts in the still frigid air, like rolling balls of yarn. Winds from the west or the south. Shadows passing over the trees, the gardens. Irises, tulips, wallflowers, periwinkles.

    The rosebush's leaves shudder and beat their wings against the wall. The scent of irises.

The trees are already full, the chestnuts' banners unfurled. I would have liked to surprise their opening and soon it will be too late. Even the oaks are budding.

Those banners trembling against the walls. Today I can picture more clearly the transition from spring to summer in the garden, during which the garden gradually closes in on itself and covers itself, changing into a pavilion or grotto of leaves, whereas in winter everything is open: iron lattice, latticework of bare branches, and the dusty ground, and the stones, with just a few grey plants, lavender, cotton lavender, candytuft. Grey, brown, white, wood, stone, iron, earth. Then the brief moment—March—comes, when pink or white butterflies flutter their wings amidst this bare, elementary matter, a moment of brief fire and light snow as if suspended in the air above the dust; and already the greenery reappears, like a humming that sets in here, then there, following some immutable order. It is the greenery of privets and climbing roses along with that of peach and almond trees, then the persimmon, glossy, almost yellow, then the fig tree. Later still comes the acacia, particularly light and trembling, finally the linden. It's still not much: the beauty of the rose leaves fluttering against the old warm stones, leaves scarcely heavier than the shadows, and hardly any more distinct, like an unceasing animation against the wall's ancient calm, like a whispered conversation. But I remember what it will become—especially in May, before the heavy, dry

heat—when space closes in and covers itself, bends
without ever being weighed down, becomes a house of
leaves and flowers, the most beautiful shelter against
expansiveness.

☙

Speak of a waning power, follow vanished poetry.
Fidelity and defiance.

☙

Mountain: ermine in flight.
    Frozen, snapping banner.
River: daughter of the arc, stemming from the arc
towards rings of the sea's target. The arc is its source.

☙

The desperate felicity of words, desperate defence of the
impossible, of that which everything contradicts, denies,
undermines or destroys. At every moment, it's like the
first and last word, the first and last poem, confounded,
solemn, improbable or without force, stubborn fragility,
persistent fountain; at night once more it sounds against
death, cowardice, stupidity; once more its freshness, its
clarity against drivel. Once more the unsheathed star.

☙

Now I side with the unattainable
and pledge once more my ageing hand
to the ever-receding target,
to arrows so fleet they glow with golden fire.
Dying, I now speak only for the gold
and, almost nothing, for the immensity of space,
and, wretched dirt, for the raptors' spheres,
and, straw, for the strongest wind and fire.

Everything breaks, everything becomes wrinkled,
    everything is defeated,
we are born to see others fall and bleed,
he flatters who calls us wisps,
but as I crumble, I will make daylight reign.

❧

Again, this evening, once more, desperate and vain talk
directed against that which feeds it,
words born of death against death,
engendered and undone by death,
an endless, impotent buzzing of flies
against flesh's decay
and day's overarching splendour.

❧

A conversation of leaves on the stone wall,
we won't speak in the sunlight much longer,

Our backs against the warm slab, we laugh
then nothing remains but the dark or the name of
    the leaf . . .

May

Acacias in bloom at night: a fragrant torrent of honey,
in perfect harmony with the birds' first trills, with the
moon, with the screech owls' piping. White rose bush,
crown or diadem. A clear expanse, without thickness or
weight.

❧

Grey dust everywhere but for a bit of fire
and the oriole said: Who are you? What are you doing?
Nothing yet was moving towards its end.

No scents: you need the heat of the day. The first fire
towards the north-east, a pink dusting.

July

Shutters still closed, the swallows' first cries rend the sky, an ominous feeling. But when I push open the shutters, the swallows fly so high in such a vast open space that it all changes.

The moon is still visible, without light, like glass or ice: enchanted hour in the garden. Then the gold of the sun appears, almost disturbs. Sign of gold and sign of silver on either side of the sky.

&

We live under a vault of thunder . . .

August

The day averts its face even in broad daylight,
Of what is it so afraid or ashamed?

🙢

R. H. Blyth's *Haiku*,[5] essential.
Zen formula:

> *There is no place to seek the mind;*
> *It is like the footprints of the birds in the sky.*

The marvellous account of the poet Matsuo Basho's
visit to the temple where his master Buccho lived.

> *Lighting one candle*
> *With another candle;*
> *An evening of spring.* (Yosa Buson)[6]

Haiku are self-obliterating. Jacques Dupin writes: 'The
song that is its own scythe.'[7]

🙢

Homage to Jules Supervielle:

To access a realm of magic. That is rare in a work.

Certainly, all the other passages are filled with
charm and marvels. But in my view this is the high point
of his life. When he wrote:

> *We are separated*
> *Only by an aspen's shudder.*[8]

he reached the centre of his being.

❧

> *Ah, singing skylark!*
> *The tail end of the grove*
> *Is still in darkness.* (Kobayashi Issa)[9]

> *Every night from now*
> *Will dawn*
> *From the white plum-tree.* (Yosa Buson's epitaph)[10]

> *The petals of the yellow rose—*
> *Do they flutter down*
> *At the sound of the rushing water?* (Basho)[11]

These poems are wings that prevent you from collapsing.

> *How admirable,*
> *he who thinks not, 'Life is fleeting,'*
> *when he sees the lightning flash!* (Basho)[12]

I could quote pages. While reading these four volumes, it occurred to me more than once that they contained, of all the words I have ever managed to decipher, those closest to the truth.

1961

January

Each drop of rain, clearest and glistening brightest where it is heaviest; attached to the glass by its shadow, its dark tip. A very small, crystalline fruit.

March

Heart darker than the violet
(eye of the abyss, soon closed)
learn to exhale the perfume
that clears so gentle a path
through the impassable.

June

Sheep move to the summer pastures. Flocks on the promenade, waxing moon, bleating according to its light. Asses tethered to the wall. Rams, their battles, the animals in a circle, sacred scene. Night falls. Dust.

1962

March

'. . . I show him the way because he is not a god: not through the forest (the leaves are too deceptive), nor even through night (what could mean more to him than the tender and luminous night, more wonderful than these mirrors, these flames, this dark colour?). I tell him to go beyond. I don't even tell him to go but to destroy, and not to see but to close his eyes as a diver does when fear overcomes him.'

'Do not climb or descend, just destroy, seek out only the most difficult, the unbearable, the impossible: the last chance, nothing is promised or certain or even probable. He should just set out again, not stand there like a beggar, a thief, a weakling of whom I'm ashamed with-out admitting it . . .'

❧

Start from nothing. That is my law. All the rest is distant smoke.

❧

Beauty: lost like a seed, at the mercy of the winds, the storms, not making a sound, often lost, always destroyed; but still it blossoms haphazardly, here, there, fed by shadows, by the funereal earth, welcomed by profundity. Weightless, fragile, almost invisible, apparently without force, exposed, abandoned, surrendered, obedient—it binds itself to what is heavy, immobile; and a flower blooms on the mountainside. It is. It persists against noise, against folly, unwavering amidst blood and malediction, in life that cannot be assumed, cannot be lived. Thus the spirit moves in spite of everything, inevitably ridiculous, unrewarded, unconvincing. And so, therefore, one must go on scattering, risking words, lending them exactly the right weight, not giving up until the end—against, always against oneself and the world, until one manages to overcome all opposition through the words themselves—words that transcend boundaries, barriers, that break through, cross over, open and finally triumph, occasionally, in fragrance, in colour—for an instant, only an instant. That, at least, is what I cling to, uttering what is almost nothing, or saying that I will utter it, which is still a positive motion, better than immobility or retreat, refusal, renunciation. Fire, the cock, dawn: St Peter. This I remember. At the end of night, when the fire still smoulders inside and outside the sun rises and the cock crows, like the call of fire tearing itself away from night. 'And he wept bitter tears.' Fire and tears, dawn and tears.

I've said it a hundred times: I am left with almost nothing; but it's like a very narrow gate through which we must pass and nothing indicates that the space beyond it is not as vast as we have imagined. It is only a matter of passing through the gate and of it not swinging shut forever.

&

Let silent grief
At least brood on this last chance
Of light.

Let this utmost misery
Harbour the chance of flowers.

&

It's as if you could no longer speak, no longer knew how to speak. You must pass through this or risk lying, cheating.

April

Monument dedicated to the impossible. The best of one-self given in complete loss to something one will never obtain.

Flowers of peach trees offered up to the bees of fire.

No more detours: return instead like a whip to the target. One's look, one's word like a whip.

From the coals of night, on the night's black branches, this blossoming, this pink grace, and soon after the humming bees of day.

Let all who wish to, recognize in this crest what is most beautiful in the world—what man discovers when insomnia wakes him at the end of the night—and what later lifts him up, like a wing, above himself.

May

Rain on thousands of leaves and what burns deep within man. Fire, its twisting.

Hawthorn petals on the stream where toads croak 'yep'. Almost the sound of a pigsty. Crickets electrified in the grass. All of it at night, and a nightingale's first trill.

In the morning, the irises, pale blue with distant perfume. Above, the mountains.

Eight o'clock in the evening. Over the chestnut trees heavy with blossoms, over the fragrances, the emanations, the agitation, the activity, the surprising blue of the sky, at once dark and luminous, profoundly blue, much more blue than during the day, and the clouds' blinding domes.

And this water flowing in the earth in bright sunlight: the memory of a mountain stream. The water and its facets of sun, its solar blades or scales. Its signs. Burying its mirrors.

July

Sheaves of wheat placed in circles like the pedestals of altars in a pale field in the evening, as the walls take on the pink hue of a dying fire. Great straw circles, dry, brittle craters.

॰॰

I have not yet found a way to describe how this world glows at dawn, the days of sun and north wind, while the mountains are weightless and blue.

Light that rhymes, in the south wind with dust, in the north wind with river. Dusty light—mirroring, trickling light. Arid, parching light—scintillating light.

There is something to be said about this sense of radiance, of weightlessness, of transparency, about the desire to walk in these gardens, these meadows, at the base of these mountains, about this irresistible sense of paradise. It would be hard to explain. Primordial elements: morning, the freshness before the day's impending heat, perfect weather, cloudless, the east, the mountains, foliage glittering like water, the *translucent* mountains like a blue border, weightless, hardly mountains any more, just blue softness, a cradle, because their details are indistinct, a blue cloth, not even, a blue boundary, the idea of a boundary . . .

September. IBIZA

Strong wind, foam on the sea, gleaming against a dark background. Storms to the left, sun to the right, Tintoretto? A celestial stage, constantly changing.

Disappear, appear. Like these games of light. You wake from a long torpor. Fold upon fold of the sea, small snow-covered mountains, soon dissipating or reforming elsewhere, in no apparent order. Here, then there. Cold, dark mass. Sudden blossoming against the rocks. Crashing, crumbling, sounds of falling scree, avalanche of water.

Is this agitation, this instability characteristic of a small island?

Windy places with bushes flat on the ground, even the roots spread out as if in a herbarium of pink dirt. Seaweed almost silver when dry.

ॐ

This skull weighing on the shoulder, masked, dressed up in flesh. Skull and skeleton masked, adorned. The weight of the skull. Baroque conceit. The skull is not masked for long. Yet why should the skull be truer than the mask, if not because it lasts a bit longer? To last in this way is meaningless. 'Happy mask': isn't that what Juliet says to Romeo or Romeo to Juliet at the Capulets' ball?

A dream in which I say before the funeral procession: 'Pay homage to the remains of one who was a most gracious lady . . .' It's the same style.

ॐ

The motif of pink or almost purple earth beneath the trees, beneath dark trees, under vibrant or damp air, depending on the day.

Grey sea, not an expanse of water but a reservoir of coolness, not a surface or a form but a memory, a mass, a fan of waves; and the forests also, a dwelling.

Moon, birds lower than the moon. Haystacks.

Earth: to be precise, one would compare it to cocoa powder (though in searching one could find an even more precise comparison and it would be false in the emotion it evokes). A colour, rather, associated with the idea of bricks, and of fire, a pale fire, a somnolent fire that doesn't burn. Earth like a sleeping fire, spread out under the trees. This is the other exactitude, the only one that matters to me. Cicadas whose song is extinguished like electricity when the motor stops.

Noise of carts, of dump trucks on bad roads.

Evening, more spacious than noon.

Trees, offerings held just above the earth; or, according to their shapes, refuges, domes, roofs.

To see it all in an instant, then never see it again (see something else? see it differently?). To be born (in darkness). To open one's eyes, to lose one's eyes.

Almost no birds: swallows, swifts, already gathered into flocks, ready to migrate. And those dogs of Egypt, from sarcophagi, thin, pale, stray. Fast. Having escaped the tombs.

Notable figures buried with their dreams, their treasures.

Invisible fires, the most intense. Nonetheless, they exist in their fashion, like that which is between things but becomes visible only when the things it binds are transformed or glorified.

Perhaps souls also abide this way, like these fires, working in secret.

Those fires, those chains. Such are the distances from one tree to the next, from one boat to the next. A first star appears because the light is fading as a veil is lifted. The sky, its colour, seems to deepen, to soften into a velvety pink, grey, violet. The star seems to shine in an immense cloud of smoke, of perfume.

Skies of ashen blackness. The idea of ash above pine trees shaking their branches, tips almost yellow, luminous against the menacing background.

Their response to the stubborn, monotonous wind: full of grace, trembling slightly, but mostly calm, patient in any case, discreet, elegant. A constant shivering, untiring, barely surrendering, turning weakness into charm. This response is more varied with the olive tree, clumsier with the carob. All these phrases hovering just above the ground, animated by an invisible threat, requiting terror with beauty.

October

Light like dust: autumn
Or, on the contrary, a mirror.

ॐ

As if you entered another space: a gentle realm that
calls to you—like a siren—that offers suggestions,
advice just when it seemed you were faced with nothing
but reefs . . .

ॐ

Flowers of another colour, of a particular colour, bloom
in autumn as the leaves grow lighter and change. Old
colours, aged—like rust, a dying fire. Season of mush-
rooms, their smell, produced by the rain—resembling
sponges, molluscs (slugs that emerge after the rain),
fragile, usually colourless or else the colour of rats, earth,
wood. Plants hidden, as if pushed out of sight, half-
buried in piles of wet leaves, mostly very light with a
delicate white stem (white things that live in the earth:
larvae, the link between mushrooms and ghosts, but fog
too), and with those hats, those wheels with fine parti-
tions, like the pages of a concentric book, like tiny

pressed wings . . . but one should not take description too far. You long to walk through forests. Under the moon night is but motionless smoke, cold, damp suspense. The traveller in his car—who passes through the world as if he were driving within a dream—either his torments will abate, if he has any, or if he is happy, his happiness will be fed by this illusion of weightlessness. A secret appears in these hills without losing its secrecy.

Hölderlin, in a letter from Hauptwyl: *Hier in dieser Unschuld des Lebens, hier unter den silbernen Alpen . . .* (*Here, in this innocence of life, here among the silvery Alps . . .*). For me, the essence of the poet is contained in the beginning of that sentence which has the same purity as a few, rare passages in *A Season in Hell*: '*Sometimes I see in the sky . . .*' This refers to a pallor that is the opposite of the mushrooms' whiteness. Angels and larvae, angels and ghosts. But it is whiteness all the same.

Colours: born of evil? White as the absence of colour, or death; white as the essence of colour, or, perhaps, of life transcended.

≥♠

Things can fall apart again at any moment. I can barely hold on to them, if I hold their shadows. What I devour like a desirable meal is perhaps no more than absence.

≥♠

Forest paths under foliage thick, dark and damp. The chill of evening matches the white or silver in the sky. The iron of cold or rather of glass.

પ્ર

In a tear—the source, perhaps—and round it if it runs, if it falls: the forest, the constellations.

I no longer know if I truly saw the tear or who shed it.

પ્ર

That smoke is in the light but an instant, that memory of fire, that farewell hovering an instant over the earth, over the room, my only knowledge—and I can hardly advance any more. The feather that symbolizes flight or a nest.

The forest must have burnt. Nothing is left but these plumes that will turn to rain.

Wool, scent.

પ્ર

Those last pink petals, the colour of exquisite shame, of secret fire, the earth's confessions. While the garden is consumed without flames, turns yellow, brown, dries out. The stems break. The hidden earth will become visible again. The trees, the vines are not tinged with gold but with the colour of a very clear flame, and yet it brings a sense of rest, not heat. Yellow . . . What had blended in with the grasses and other plants now becomes *distinct*, alters and reveals itself, hastening towards its end. It reveals itself and its fragility, its frailty. It admits it has become worn out, frayed, torn, stained. How difficult it is to grasp the essential! It is tempting to go too far or not far enough, to be too vague or too precise. Things should be grasped suddenly but exactly, like a gunshot. There are, in fact, hunters in these yellowed vineyards—gun smoke, birds suddenly take flight, baying—a threat of fog, a kernel of it in the sunlit air. When the foliage thins, the birds are endangered. Autumn bears the colours of feathers, of fur, of foxes and dogs. Autumn looks less like plants. The trees disguise themselves, put on costumes. Fatal celebration, mournful in a way. The trees are like roosters—in air turning cold, under a sun growing pale. They also resemble the October sun: pale yellow, then deep red when it sinks into the haze over the horizon. Colours of pheasants. And the clouds like being pink above these aviaries, these farmyards. The spirit enjoys such days when the forests become lighter, barer, when a softness in the air persists round a cold core. It suddenly perceives a few trees at dawn, like a bouquet in the mist, like gems on a bed of cotton batting, like a sun of leaves in the clouds, like a jewel in the linens.

෧

You can no longer discern things clearly.
Thrown back into incomprehension,
Your last thoughts are jumbled,
Your world reduced to the movement of a wind that
  blows early.

&

New world
no longer of thoughts
nor of axioms to be developed peacefully until
  your death
but a pavilion of pictures
protected from space not by a wall
but by visions.
There is no longer any question of dwelling on
  firm ground
You are carried away,
You now possess only what is fleeting.
All that is certain is extinguished like a lamp snuffed out
You rush towards a source that has fled
You are fed by the morning wind.

December

Again, before day, that restfulness, that blue, that divine eye. And the earth covered with frost, as if in retreat, as if shut away, like worm-eaten wood.

Then the dusting of gold, the mist, these hills like boats in the mist.

A flock of pigeon circles above a distant farm.

લ્જ

An extinguished lamp—the rain's tomb.

A lamp, suddenly extinguished. What its light was in the darkness, when the others are no longer lit.

લ્જ

That pink hue at night on or in the mountains, that fire. Almost like glances, fervour. Under a sky of endless blue.

લ્જ

Night, and before it flees, its fringes, its fiery mottling.

લ્જ

In winter, before dawn, between the mountains and the dark clouds, on the black silhouettes of the trees like poles, tatters of pale orange or mauve flags (at night they will be pink) announce the army of light.

1963

January

I had a mirror
In which I no longer saw my face
But eyelids closed over embers
A profound world of pink.

I shall have to shatter it
Before it has hidden the air.

ح

Oh, the fire that spreads again at dawn
Born of the horizon's sleep
And in the frost's spittle on the windowpanes
The fire blazes because the mountains have lain down
And closed their eyes.
A fire starts in the blue of sleep
Dreaming mountains
In love.

ح

Flowers.

They sprout among the bones in the subterranean
house of the dead, or else in the land of dreams, in a thick

mass with fire in its core. The earth itself, a fruit with a kernel of flame, hanging beneath its foliage of clouds.

Ice, blades, leaves of frost. You can still see these things, or you no longer perceive them as things but as emanations, ideas, tropes, movements, births.

Sometimes the entire world seems like a bubble, a flurry of snow that only our eyes think is motionless or weighty.

❧

I will spend the night in this boat. No lantern on the bow or the stern. Nothing but a few stars in the pearly water and the drowsy movement of the current. I will head for a dubious shore, following the beacon of the first, frightened birds' rare cries.

Souls taken from the world, why not hope for a similar landing place? There are perhaps some cries as yet unknown, a look that nothing stops, that cannot exhaust anything—something that surpasses all knowledge, all imagination, all desire?

❧

During those long, deep frosts, buried in earth turned hard as rock, flower buds in their capsules, their sheaths.

Birds drawn close to the houses.

❧

Black waterfall suspended
Mysterious, equine
Plumage
Something to twist
Burning close to our centre
Mane, firebrand, inverted torch
Night's flame by day
Iron in our heart

March

First buds, first leaves
Nights that grow larger and lighter
Violets, why
So dark, so perfumed?

May

The light has been removed from the trees' lantern

&

Everything has been pushed back into another world
Frontier
I will not cross it again
Someone is walking on the other side
Or did I dream it?
I follow the footsteps all night
By day, I can hardly advance

June

In the flowering linden tree
beyond its fullness
and its humming
the view
the evening sky
light's flight

Only that still wakes me
this distant sleep

Nothing but the luminous air
and somewhere the sleeping fire
Nothing but this today
the immense world
the house of birds
and the nest of sleep

September

At night, the trees and the gardens are caught in a wash-house steam, though cold, and, above them, stars. Then, in the morning, beautiful weather hatches from this nest of fog.

❧

Poplars, guardians of shade, backlit in the hovering day.

1964

January

Winter so fittingly named with the fleet bird's name
Season clear and bare
More direct than any other
Season arched like a bow
Time of birds gathered together
From the high, aerial nets
Mother of pearl and earth
Glass and straw

❧

Shadow that emerges from anywhere, that tears or corrupts.

Things torn from the world, the world's wounds.

A cart moving slowly along the road, carrying dead things, a fragment of time—tattered, it lingers in your memory, sweet and cruel, until memory itself is carried away, commemoration forgotten.

❧

All visible things—like the screams or sighs of the Invisible suffering from being invisible, like little flames rising from or hovering round a furious (or happy) conflagration. What is it being born so slowly with such torment? What is the fundamental and profound event of which we can only perceive multiple emanations, infinite projections? And from what common seed do these birds, these beads of sweat, these stones endlessly emerge? Sometimes it seems that fissures suddenly yawn open before us, as if created by lightning, their direction pointing towards a centre, and if something in us reverberates or rumbles like an auspicious vibration, it's already another day, another night and it all may end before anything comes of it . . . Everywhere we read signs, but the eye that discerns them is ready to close, and the signs remain scattered, fitful as birdcalls before dawn. Dust blown by the wind or breath fallen back onto the table; night is full of bright dust. Why did this kernel open? From which other kernel came the force that allowed it to burst open? Of what treasure are we the scattered and degraded remains?

Where will this abyss that yawns open now and again lead us? What is this icy shadow in the light of the expanding year, in the warming day?

Appearances, like so many pleas. Will this torment be a twisting that refines or smothers?

❧

The hamlet of Teyssieèrs, near the source of the Lez, with its pure water. On the Lance's steep eastern face, now darkened, pines mingle with other trees, like dark pink fans. At the bottom of a combe, a river runs beneath ice. The earth is moist, heavy, cold. Boxwood and mulberry trees grow along the road. The hamlet, in shivering, snowy shade, resembles a lost pig farm, inhabited only by old men. In the windows, against a backdrop of soot, you can see their faces, stupid or haggard.

 є

Parmenides
—*At night a borrowed light wanders round the earth.*
—*Eternally turned towards the bright rays of the sun.*
—*The earth rooted in water.*

Empedocles
—*And the rain, mother of the dark and the cold . . .*
—*Creatures hard and compact when in their shells and soft when outside it, shaped by the hands of* Cypris *from wetness.*
—*As when a man, contemplating a journey through a winter night, lights a lantern . . .*
—*And the black colour on the bottom of a river arises from the shadow and appears also in hollow caves.*
—*The ear, fleshy sprout in which a bell rings.*

є

A pool among rocks, under ice, in the shade. From the depths of the earth. The earth weeps.

≀▲

A scorpion crushed amidst coals in the damp cave. Many men have been treated, are treated thus. The dark, the pallid, the damp.

Vestal virgins buried alive. Plutarch's description of the litter on which they were carried.

≀▲

Like a saw cutting wood
Destruction rends the heart
Time in the thickness of the air.

≀▲

A look that closes in on itself
As if there were less water in the valleys.
Where will it reappear?

≀▲

Instead of sleeping, you must watch the night, the suffering it harbours.

Then you will deal only with the impossible, countering the impossible with the impossible. There is an extreme moment when that becomes necessary (I am not speaking of myself, only of what I intuit and what is common to us all). At that limit, only mute prayer can begin again, the soul cowering in apprehension and grief, the spirit disarmed. Only a senseless murmur can begin again, as if deprived of a place, of direction, of space, stammering from the depths. Perhaps also deprived of purpose, existing only in itself, disoriented. Against the teeth of the saw that rends. To the point at which action no longer achieves anything, when the hand can only stop and fall, powerless.

'You carried me into the light, you've torn yourself
    apart, you are undone, you can no longer carry
    anything.
You came, you leave again
You have laughed, at one with yourself, you will be
    scattered and speechless
You descend beyond our reach
You are nothing but emptiness encircled in a ring
    of tears
For a moment, the lost hearth of our thoughts
You dive where we cannot follow
In order to follow you, must we rise higher, the deeper
    you sink
Just as the sky brightens when shadows pour over the
    fields?
The deeper the wound, the gentler the balm?
That will be the path when all paths are gone

Perhaps then it will seem to me that I am carrying you,
   crushed and absent as you are, just as you carried
   me, a blind beginner.'

࿇

We hear moaning, as if someone were bearing too heavy
a weight of pleasure or pain. Ploughing. Like someone
possessed by a nocturnal fit of violence. You were
thrown to the ground, you are still, but by an opposite
force, just as the void is set against fullness and ice
against fire.

   Who has mistreated you so? You were a fragrant
fire, now you are broken and trembling. You will be
thrown out with the refuse, hidden in the earth. Your
beauty misled the spirit; it cannot bear the horror of your
demise, not even from a distance, in thought.

࿇

The opening of Duc de Saint-Simon's memoirs: a world
in which the ridiculousness of a bad dancer can be con-
sidered *prodigious*.

࿇

Monteverdi: the flame that becomes ornament without
ceasing to burn. More than any other, this music evokes
the idea of fire, of night and stars. This relates both
to Shakespeare and to Titian (the Vienna *Danaë*, for

example). Yet, rather than a golden rain falling on nudity, it is as if a transforming power in these melodies were rising from the substance of her body, its velvety, painted density, up to the highest point in the heavens, a power one could almost *grasp* in certain arabesques, like the one that ornaments the word *stele* in *Ed è pur dunque vero*, or the word *prezzo* in the *Lettera amorosa* (the text of which, as a matter of fact, plays on hair that is both a flame and a golden shower). These figures, like flowers blooming, are always tied to the subterranean world of passion. Similarly, no music is better suited to the text of Torquato Tasso's *Battle of Tancredi and Clorinda*, so voluptuous despite its uplifting ending.

Rereading the beginning of Saint-Simon's memoirs, I am struck most of all by the intrusion of base or repellent details in an account so preoccupied with reverence and rank: the bursting of the urn containing internal organs, the Duc de Richelieu's enemas. As if Paulo Veronese had slipped an incongruous object in the corner of his lavish scenes, the emanations of which could profane any ceremony.

Speaking costs the lips so little
But I will press them to the wound

If that is the only way
I will rot without being able to pass
Through the mouldering eye of the needle.

February

This slight disturbance of the air announces spring too
soon, like a melting of light.

ॐ

This light in the yellow earth, in the earth's straw, this egg.
As if a white bird were ascending.

ॐ

Birds taking flight from trees shaken by the wind.
Internal light, world, illuminated forest . . .

And yet, we were done wrong
and a tear forms at the base of the wound
already somewhat consoling
All this light, could it not be an immense tear?
It is the eyes that weep, because they see
Because they are the ones that create lasting tears.
We perceive the site of our life through two tears.

ॐ

Birds peeping in the raging wind, like a fear, like dis-
traught, agitated bubbles.

Last night, surprised by the light of early spring—most of all because it has started to linger—by the fact that we could still see clearly at seven o'clock; at the same time, we could see brilliant stars. The wet asphalt shone too. Perhaps there was already more green. We could describe, and describe again . . . the surprise, the emotion arose from a centre more hidden, more primitive than description.

What does that god—the one who seems to inhabit the secret, the depths, and who asks nothing, demands nothing, that convenient god—have to do with Jesus Christ, the most difficult god? The god of the secret presentiment is not moral but he feels closer to me than the other.

June

Everything is less easy now
Gentleness is almost forgotten
We are more careful with words
Now the flight falters
The wing limps
There is a weight on my neck
And I hardly dream any more
In other words
I could now use a good slap.

૨૧

On a postcard from Venice, a marvellous detail from
Tintoretto's paining of Arianna and Bacchus. It is prob-
ably Arianna's head, bent, in profile, against a sunset sky
turning from golden pink to blue green. In her hair the
wave joins the flame and a hand holds over her head, not
yet setting it down, a thin crown decorated with stars we
believe we really can see glittering.

૨૧

The joy of clarity.

Concerning the journal *Hermes*, numbers 1 and 2.

By returning periodically to the *immediate*, I am drawn to the editors' main concern. For example, in the collection of the monk Hakuin's writings entitled *Conversation in a Boat at Dusk*, what I find most striking is the account of his journey: how, since there are no roads, he follows the sound of the river, the old man's silence, the stain in the fog that is a bank of reeds, the purity of the air, a sense of oppressiveness. In light of these themes, medical theories become tedious, infinitely distant from me.

The drama is in the relation of the immediate to what is mediated, which Henri Michaux articulates (*Le dépouillement par l'espace/Divestment by Space*). There is also the danger of egotism. In this respect, Chassidism is more humane, more mindful of the *other*.

Hermann Broch's gloss on Hugo von Hofmannsthal's letter to Lord Chandos overlooks an important aspect. In the very throes of his crisis, something remains: 'a watering can, a harrow left in the field . . . can become the vessel of my revelation.' This sheds light on modern poetry. '[R]ather a . . . shepherd's fire . . . than the majestic roar of an organ.' The unified and lasting is broken; only fragments remain and, between them, an almost unbearable void that threatens to engulf them.

July

A farm beneath large oaks: harrow, grinding wheel, blue cart, barrel hoops. Shadow and wind.

Further off, in front of wheat and lavender fields, poplars standing in circles of shade round their bases (noon).

෴

Downslopes of skin. Archers.

Do not look at this from outside. This is not some performance, it is something experienced deeply, something you have gone through, the secret in which you live, from which you cannot stand apart.

When you are in the body, at the heart of the world—when you are no longer a glance, even when you look at something, your glance is trapped within it.

Only when imprisoned are you alive, not when you are set free.

In these sweat-soaked chains, polished, smooth.

Longing for these chains, for this blinding

In this shadowy and gleaming water, in this cage of sighs

Bath

As though inside a fruit . . .

᷒

Fig: fire enveloped in night, or else a kind of sponge, of
        spongy pink coral
Always just before decay sets in.
Hornets frantically coupled.

᷒

Mown fields, bordered by a semi-circle of trees; it
suddenly arrests your glance. It is a site. The invisible is
hidden in its centre.

September

Fog at dawn, muffled shots, pigeons flying at an angle
as if they were scaling heights.

October

Fierce winds: yellow leaves suddenly take flight. Fleet black clouds eclipse the sun for a moment. Always white birds in the distance, doves. Their colour, in the bed of the wind, the bed of time, while we get older, suffer or are afraid of disasters, the mere thought of which is unbearable. No truth beyond this?

Children, as vulnerable as these leaves.

November

Seven in the morning: chestnut trees like a flame in the mist; the green of the grass between the stocks of vine, intense and clear. Hard to grasp what it is that the strangeness of these trees evokes (from which the cries of birds still come.) Aggressive car engines. A hunter, hunched and skinny, passes quickly, engraved by Jacques Callot.

1965

January

A walk in fine, clear weather. An area where, in other
years, the flooding river left behind long stretches of
pebbles and mud with dead wood. A dyke protects the
fields. You can see snow on Mont Ventoux, on the hills.
In the shelter of the embankment, a meadow with three
poplars and beyond that, rows of cypresses protect the
ploughed fields. Further still, a thicket of tall aspen,
sawed-off trunks at their feet, an assembly of large white
stones: once again a site with an almost sacred combi-
nation, mysterious and touching, in any case, natural ele-
ments under a pure, wavering light. In the cage of trees,
in their web, under their sparse enchantment. Limbs of
water that are not dead, a shiver brings the surface to
life, and the water is clear, too—no algae, no crawling
things. Winter's wing.

April

Whiteness of the bushes, the fruit trees, if you think of it as snow that emerges from the earth instead of falling towards it.

August

Passers-by seen as flames.

❧

The fig tree's movement at night under the moon. On such a calm night, it seems as though you need only wait for a wind to rise at any moment, as light as a breath, to rustle the leaves on the vine and those of the fig tree, making a noise at once soft and crackling, dry, like paper. Then you see the fig tree, completely black, moving slowly, serenely. For a moment, because of this slight movement in the vast silence, it seems to contain the world. The silence is unusual, not a single car passes, not one dog barks. It's as though you begin to see again. Once again, a tree seems an utterly incomprehensible thing.

❧

The landscape of the Lance, valleys planted with lavender. The lavender plants are harvested. Sickles. Cut, they form grey bundles, almost black, the colour of slate, in the field of stones.

The ravines are probably arid. Then forests, filled mostly with beech, with raspberry bushes, mulberry trees, briar rose, large bushes of blue thistle, and above a scree of grey rocks, cut sheer, like hard paving stones on the path. Box tree and crickets. Almost no birds. On the ascent is a sloping glade with a ruined house and a stream; like a park with slopes facing the hills near and far, rendered beautiful by exposure and unexpected essences: willow and pine. But what retains you most is a sense of 'cleanness', an absolutely natural cleanliness (not in any way tended or forced), at once soft and pure, clear cut, without debris: meadows like model lawns. This strange simplicity holds you for a long time, in the evening, in complete silence and perfect clarity.

The folds in the expanse are harmonious, neither losing nor breaking their shape, blanketed by the forests' shade.

Further down, in a valley filled with the same cleanness that reigns in the park round the farmhouse, the sheep on the hillside look like ant eggs.

September

Impossible: having to read about the same events in the newspapers every day is, strictly speaking, unendurable. It seems impossible to go on, and yet you do. How?

Because poetry can help you face down the unendurable. Face down—that is perhaps an overstatement.

What makes expressing myself difficult today is that I do not want to cheat—and it seems to me that most people cheat, more or less, with their own experiences. They put it in parentheses, cover it up.

At that point certain words should enter into poetry, words it has always avoided, been wary of, and yet without moving towards naturalism, which, in its own way, is also a lie. There is an area between Samuel Beckett and Saint-John Perse at opposite extremes, each systematic in his own way.

But then one is always just inches from the impossible.

છ.

The enchantress is now without power. The doors no longer open.

She suffers from it. Used up, she screams. Her screams are sorrow, her rage suffering.

The days are the instruments that operate on her; she screams when she feels their touch.

Her shelter, her shields, her guardians are all taken away. It's as if she were being skinned alive.

❧

You imaginative children, how they will beat you!

❧

There is no word weighty enough or simple enough, it seems, to endure next to the unspeakable; that is the one to find.

Plough. The plough that divides man from sweetness, from light. Who leans his weight upon it, on its handles?

So little time. Such brief periods. How can you grasp anything whatsoever? You've barely finished dreaming, before other dreamers crowd in.

❧

Eyes open, then closed again: what has been gained, what acquired, what changed, what progress made?

Let us be as abiding as animals.

❧

The precise expression, yes, if it illuminates, if it shows the way.

≈

I grope for the thread. Just as the instruments in an orchestra are tuned in disorder.

Yet there are still luminous clouds, cliffs rising up to the skies, shades of pink and violet in the stones.

≈

Perhaps we should work towards a less metaphysical mode of expression: then death turns to attentiveness, patience, fear, weakness, wounds and bandages, no grand words, not even a battle, only gestures, smiles, tears, wakefulness. No revelation: patience, suffering, anguish, wonder. Weakness above all, perhaps, the weakness of a child; a child's distress. Nothing grandiose. And yet . . .

≈

Figs and grapes, nurtured by the mountains under sluggish clouds and high, brisk skies, will they guide me for much longer as they have until now?

≈

Snows of the air, suspended glaciers at home where the sun's heat, encountering no obstacles, no longer warms anything.

❧

In the narrow streets of Riez, in the morning, between the dark, filthy four-storey houses, I could not help but think of Shakespeare's theatre. This impression struck far more forcefully than in any towns and villages in Provence that were simply charming or picturesque, often too run-down or too well kept. In Riez, something of the real sixteenth century still seemed present. It was harsh, almost sinister, chivalrous too and had an extraordinary vitality in its nobility and filth, starkly lit. I am speaking only about two long parallel streets, hidden behind the public squares and the winding alleys; streets only partially inhabited with enormous gaps, here and there a building had collapsed entirely, leaving the adjacent houses leaning over a void (thin pilasters still visible on the wall left standing). From far away, it evoked Naples rather than France in the intensity of the feeling. Elsewhere in Provence, there is instead a sense of equilibrium, of grace, etc. But the Haute-Provence still has places of an admirable wildness, lost villages in areas so harsh you would think you were in Spain.

❧

Nyons. This dark vestibule, decorated with fake marble and an antelope skin, and, next to it, a small walled gar-, den with a palm tree and fountain.

The chapel of Notre-Dame-du-Bon-Secours, built in a tower in the nineteenth century, resembles a little circus with its colourful paintings and rustic benches set close together on rising stands above the altar.

ક।

A child's voice: in a high, graceful register that evokes words like 'cowbells' and, behind them, the freshness of grass in the mountain pastures where they are heard most often at night, which is blue.

ક।

Apple trees in the orchard. That reddish purple, that waxy yellow; grasp their meaning. Low trees, laden with fruit, set close and now entangled. The shade and the grass below them. Autumn. The stream in which the walnut tree just barely dips the tips of its branches.

To speak of embers, globes of embers, as I did in one of the poems in *Airs*, is an inadequate approximation and somewhat misleading. The word 'purple' is right in one sense, but not in all. There is the roundness and the hardness of the pulp; but it's not a matter of examining everything through a magnifying glass. It must simply be grasped *in passing* and *from afar*, with *immediacy and depth*. Ultimately, I am not particularly concerned with the *tree's essential quality*, which Francis Ponge studied so superbly well. In the blink of an eye, you grasp a combination of elements, but not on an abstract or general level because other essences will have a similar, but not identical, effect. There is the idea of fire, like a fire slumbering in the nest of leaves; there is the idea of a globe, of roundness, of a sphere, that of fruit in general. But particular to the apple tree is perhaps some ruggedness, peasant rusticity, something untidy rather than harmonious, irregular, in any case, rough, simple, common. The opposite of the exoticism or luxury that other fruit trees might evoke here, nothing biblical like the fig tree. It's the European countryside, so childhood too, parents, home. Something central. *Domestic* trees. Maids. Farm maids. So you should associate what is near with what is far, the transient with the permanent, the unusual and the common—and all in a moment of vitality and insouciance, not through discipline, insistence, toil, etc. All the research should vanish. In passing, while the spirit was worried about something else, or in despair even, a sign was given, a gift.

૨**ଈ**

Persistent worry, better called fear, about the future. And yet autumn opens like a cradle, you feel you are suspended in the white light, warm and unmoving, amidst the grapes that grow heavier and darker, the figs that ferment, covered with wasps and flies. How can you free yourself?

ề.

One more day of this blinding suspension. Trembling carcase in this soft, luminous space.

Blue lavender flowers with a yellow centre, violet blue, pink mauve, in cascading bouquets. Large yellow flowers amidst dark greens, their intensity, which the word 'suns' does not quite capture, once again. An indecipherable yellow that still must be deciphered as if to be fortified.

Children untied in sleep.

October

A fire of leaves that smells of horses, of stables.

In the morning, the earth is covered with haze, as if smoking, which I associate with the word 'washhouse'. In L. it was located in the strange quarter near the tunnel; a poor, crowded neighbourhood, with small shops and vaguely dubious cafes, warehouses, maybe a sawmill. Lots of those small balconies inseparable from the ornate architecture of the early twentieth century on which almost no one ever stands. There was a swimming pool at the washhouse where the gym teacher was meant to have taught me to swim in winter. My associations with this place have always had a touch of the sinister and suspect in the smells and steam of the laundry.

❧

The wonderful beginning of the *Purgatorio* and, in Canto II, the angel's appearance with white wings. Then Casella begins his poem and extreme gentleness comes over the pilgrims. Inimitable chasteness and a purity of tone that allows only minor variations.

At the opening of Canto XIII, those voices, those phrases suspended in the air, cut short.

❧

Forest of holm oak: their colour, the colour of light in their shadow and in them, apparently elusive; the pale green lichen on their trunks. Delve deeper.

The swollen river, agitated: it carries away the milk of winter.

As the light weakens, the leaves become sparse.

❧

Winter, like beautiful wood, like an old piece of furniture.

1966

February

The wind does not even disturb the columns of smoke.
The almond tree blossoms.

March

The small pink peach tree in the distance, in a corner of the light green meadow. Nothing else, an arrow that digs into our very core.

૨**

The radiance that shines from some of Joseph Joubert's thoughts, from Étienne Pivert de Senancour's (those of the latter among a much-too-diffuse jumble of reflections and complaints).

૨**

Joubert: 'This globe is a drop of water; the world is a drop of air. Marble is thickened air.' 'Only water that falls from the sky can survive in drops and shine like the dew.' 'Our life is of woven wind.'

And the beautiful passage in which Obermann bends over the flowers: 'If flowers were beautiful only in our eyes, they would still be seductive; but sometimes their perfume enjoins us like fortunate conditions in life, or a sudden call, to return to a more intimate life . . .' Through all these years, I have hardly thought of anything but such a return, drawn by the call of things that to me too never seemed '*merely* beautiful'.

੨®

After I spoke to V. about my dream of harmonizing the best and the worst in a poem, the subtle Professor B. told me he believes such dreams are impossible today. He prefers my prose narrative 'Obscurity' to my poems. Yet more and more often I hear the lies of speech which paralyse me. I wish misery would expose them. This is just a wish. I am neither uncouth nor simple.

April

Insomnia: dread at the thought of certain lives I've watched unfold from very near since childhood, lives that seemed almost heroic at first, brilliant in any case, and are ending in the inescapable despair of illness. Men once so sure of themselves, puffed up with vanity over vague honours—men who have collapsed pitifully. After this, having risen very early, I welcome the day's water and all this darkness is washed away.

May

A field of sainfoin, not really pink, but nearly the colour of earth, of an ember almost extinguished. Nightingales in all the bushes.

A crown of white roses. The sparse, untidy hair of an old man with a serious illness—that is what I thought of this year at the sight of the large rosebush. At the moment I'm still thinking of King Lear in the storm. He has no strength left; the slightest odour is a torment to him even though he was the least squeamish of men.

❧

One of Borges' texts written in 1930, 'The Superstitious Ethics of the Reader', develops a theme that is unexpected from so subtle a stylist: 'The perfect page, the page in which no word can be altered without harm, is the most precarious of all.'[13] He foresees the time when (hasn't it already come?) literature will 'court its own demise' by becoming mute. He opposes Cervantes to Góngora.

I had a similar sentiment when I read the passage in Ponge's *Pour un Malherbe*, in which he has no qualms about elevating Malherbe and Góngora above Cervantes and Shakespeare.

❧

Tall grasses one evening after long hours of rain. Gardens invaded by plants, over walls already leaning towards the ground. You feel even more enclosed— under the clouds, in the mist, the trees appear larger or denser. A stream clouded with mud runs along the park, there where you can enter over a rusted iron footbridge.

❧

The perfume of flowers: smelling an iris or a rose is the only gesture that immediately takes me back to my childhood; and not as if remembering one of the moments, but as if transported there for the length of a lightning flash. It's strange that the presence of an age already long past is connected to what is most fragile and invisible, to the breath of such ephemeral beings.

❧

I better understand the movement of mountains: at once a slow ascension and concentration. Furthermore, if I say 'mountain', the thing is there as is the idea, tangible or not; whereas the word 'ascension', in its abstraction, deprives the idea of life and therefore of the fullness of its truth. Perhaps that is the weakness in what is called abstract painting: the wish to make explicit what was previously hidden, modestly and sometimes unconsciously, in other styles.

❧

The rejoinder is that in this day and age it's no longer possible to feign innocence, that we must work (paint, write) *with* all the knowledge that burdens our consciousness. Still, some ignorance remains, whatever we do, always as much. That is what Ungaretti wrote in his text for Michaux.

❧

The extreme timidity of birds. Shying away at the slightest disruption of their habits.

❧

Why would we have drunk the day's water every morning?

❧

A walk in the long evening. Tall grasses under leafy trees. Aged stones. Wells and fountains like old tombs—or altars—sometimes in the shade of an almond tree but also old tombs or monuments like fountains.

❧

Link between soul and ugliness. The love-act of plants, of insects. It only begins to seem shameful (from outside) between higher animals. The same is true of wounds, illness, etc. If we do approach things, then it's because of a dream of innocence, as for a baptism.

What place should we accord the ignoble? The honour of a superior status? What do we reach through wounds? Wound of the eyes.

Baptized anew every morning by the day.

Bouquets of jasmine. I live in a Greek country.

୬

The tree's shadow on flowers in bloom.

୬

I now have that shadow of pain behind me no matter what I write. It makes all the poems I've written seem too fluid and almost every sentence as well. Because no word is pain; on the contrary, it is detached, intact.

A wounded light, as I imagine it in front of the Rembrandt in Cologne, is that not Christ? We could no longer believe in an intact god. It did not suffice. But in a god whose wounds alone are visible? And so, in turn, I discover myself between the young Greek gods and the crucified god, between the gods of youth and the gods who were to come only once mankind felt old and ill. I have changed much less than I thought. Once again I have returned with a candle to old Madame G.'s bedside in the large room with closed shutters. I do nothing but repeat the same thing over and over; if only it could become more and more true.

❧

Birds fed with worms. Able to fly for having eaten of the earth.

❧

Whatever ties us in this landscape to the ancient and elemental is the source of its grandeur, whereas in other landscapes these images (sometimes just illusions, but significant nonetheless) are less present or altogether absent. We see this especially in the worn stone, spotted with lichen, close to fur or plants, bark; the walls that have for the most part become useless in the woods; the wells; the houses invaded by ivy and abandoned. At this point in history, when man is further removed from the elemental than ever before, these landscapes, in which man-made monuments can barely be distinguished from the rocks and the earth, shake us to the core and feed the dream of return in time, which appeals to many who are frightened by the strange future taking shape. We recognize that there isn't much difference between the Alyscamps and the abandoned quarries of Saint-Restitut, which in turn remind us of the Forum. We feel that these wells and canals—perhaps dug by the Romans, perhaps dug much later, it doesn't matter—connect us to a pagan mystery. Is it just a game? Or an escape? It still seems there are columns scattered round us here and there, and traces of temples. What does this mean and what will it profit us or teach us? We come upon, we often cross over, *places* that have disappeared completely elsewhere. What is a *place*? A kind of centre put in relation to a whole. No longer an area set apart, lost, futile. On this spot, long ago, they had built altars, set up stones. The Val des Nymphes proves this. In such a place, there is communication between worlds, between the high and the low; and because it is a centre, we don't feel the need to leave it. A restfulness reigns there, a contemplativeness.

Perhaps our church is this enclosure with crumbling walls where oaks grow silently, crossed once in a while by a rabbit or a pheasant. We are hesitant to enter other churches because of the intellectual frameworks they interpose between us and the divine. That, of course, is no way out of any difficulty.

It seems to us that in a world woven entirely of such places, we might still have been willing to accept the risk and yield. These places help us; there is a reason more and more people seek them out, often without knowing why. They can no longer bear being alienated from space. Only in such places do they feel they can breathe again and believe life is possible. We have, in a way, benefited from their gifts and have fashioned an existence for ourselves less false than many others. But that brings with it a strange aloofness from present concerns and more than one danger. In any case, let us acknowledge our privileges.

Innocence and culture: the best in culture always maintains a reflection of original innocence and is not its opposite. The works we love are also connected to 'places', even if they are of a different order, etc. The only true culture is the one that preserves and passes on innocence, the native. All else should be given another name.

The good is nested in our silence; the power to break it ripens in our isolation.

୬

We are accompanied by bending shadows
The more you advance, the more the tool digs into
    your skin
We are filled with futile pity
A tree of sadness grows deep within us
Nothing is harder than not anticipating one's death
When it seems that all one can expect is
Still more weakness and pain.

୬

And yet one is still in the freshness, in the light
The ability to do a bit of good is not lost
One can still change one's life at any moment
With much attention and gentleness.
(Constantly altering the course of things
At least as long as there is still time.
Later, others will hold firm.)

≥⬥

At the limit of his exhaustion
What does he carry?
He collapses onto his shadow
Saturated with pity.
Rot attacks his words
He no longer knows how to keep it from creeping into
    his heart
Now there are no more places
Words are like routed soldiers
What power could regroup them?
No magic can help any more.
Torments, infinite or far off, grow like mountains.

≥⬥

For a long time I kept wounds at bay
With the flights of birds
Air and feathers surrounded me
For now my skin is still intact
But they have entered into me
Sometimes they bleed, especially at night
I can still see the birds
But I bleed while they fly
When I only hear them
Without seeing them, at the heart of the day
I feel a little spared.

June

The long evenings are warmer, the moon pink or orange, the world blue, suspended, full of gentleness.

Full of horror.

❧

Truly full of gentleness and as if of goodness. These nights of full moon, more yellow than pink or orange, when the trees seem to breathe because of the weak wind, are like a balm. Their warmth and calm unbind the heart. The slow, imperceptible rise of the wheat-coloured orb; breath of leaves; crickets and owls, nightingales, the only remaining sounds. Let us bathe in this milky water, even if only for a moment, before it expels us. Let us sleep or speak in this airy cradle.

❧

The sky is recharging now; the air is sultry. That is all it takes for the hand to release its grip. When you are constantly struck from afar, whether by threats or images, you grow tired. And yet you hear a child's clear voice, touch his perfect, cool skin. Later, everything that is shadow or suffering will surprise and sadden him. You tremble for his coming days.

You think you are immobile, yet you slowly descend. Turn this fall into an ascent.

❧

Already, the grasses in the field are dried-out. Like feathers: light, almost white, straw-coloured, almost invisible stalks slightly higher than thicker grasses, and always moving, though without a sound. Light and sere, like skeletal grass. Feathery crests, weightless plumes. Fields extending to the low walls, either trembling or solid.

❧

The water of thoughts: words to wash the soul.

❧

The emotional charge of words is probably stronger, the more hidden it is. What Marc Chagall said to me of Mozart: Tthe more transparent his music, the more you can sense death. I'm not sure those were his exact words, but there is truth and beauty in that thought. The law of contradiction: the more literature aspires to be pure inspiration, the more verbal it seems (surrealism). Which doesn't mean that it must be verbal to seem inspired.

❧

Keep things in their rightful place and do not let death encroach needlessly on life. The necessity, the blessing of limits (rereading Michaux with undiluted admiration).

Let these limits be like the old walls in fields and in forests: aged, humane, not evoking a standstill or closure as much as a kind of justice and order without pedantry, fruitful. *Barricades mystérieuses*. Fertile measure.

≥❧

In this year when the crown of white roses
Reminded me of sparse, unkempt hair
On the brow of an old man resigned to his suffering
    with sad courage
And of the old king in the storm
Men so worthy by virtue of their years and humble
    knowledge
Next to whom youth seems foolish and raucous . . .
If we could have a fraction of such wisdom and
    courage
Rather than too much useless knowledge and too
    many dreams.
We lose them and yet they accompany us still.
The light lasts longer than the lamp
So that the chain of clarities is not broken.
Now that I have seen death, it fascinates me less than
    before I knew it
I'd like to turn away from it as from something incom-
    plete and, perhaps, meaningless.

It seems to me that the light has grown today
Like a plant.

~

I now want only to remove
that which keeps us from the light
leaving room only
for the heart's ripening fruit.
I listen to old men
who are in tune with the day
I learn patience at their feet.

~

Quarries, caverns, faults in the ground, fallen rocks,
sand. Fields thick with wheat invading the hillsides like
a tide.

~

Goodness pierces us, exposes. Cruelty confines. Link
between eroticism and theatre: red, black and gold. The
Marquis de Sade's castle.

~

The child says she is thinking, at night, of sad things, of
her parents' deaths. They are like swift birds in her sky;
their shadows fall on her games, on her beginning.

July

Lavender interspersed with high grasses almost white they are so dry or with flowering umbels. Your glance lingers. Plumes or milky spots in cradling sleep, in the waters of night?

❧

Pure, motionless evenings; and there is one moment when, above the fans of irrigating water, spraying in clusters, we see that the eastern sky is like silver between the leaves: just like water, when the colours have left it.

❧

If I listen to the days' sound
what will I hear
but the falling of days
into the unknown deep?
We are made of radiance, we have no more existence
than a knot of glittering water.

Life gradually changed into images, reduced to images
that filter through us.
The poet transmits the purest ones.

Our body of images, of memory.

All this trouble, sometimes these torments, these griefs
for a bubble of images. Collected within us like
seeds in the fruit.

Wounds that leave not the faintest trace in the air.

Earth that absorbs decay from the very beginning of
the world.

Settling within us, set down deep within us are images
carefully stored like a shipment of flowers. They
fall to the bottom.

Could there be anything more futile than a life with its
hoard of images—and yet we have premonitions of
another order.

So much trouble for a knot of air! So quickly, so easily
untied!

⁊☙

That's not quite accurate. 'Knot of air' is easily said. Seen
from a distance, perhaps. But in the very moment and
from up close? The most surprising thing is perhaps this:
reality is only ever the present instant. The past and the
future, stretching out on either side of this moment, are
simply collections of images. No matter how keen your
suffering, it is only of this moment; yesterday's suffering
is nothing but image.

We advance like a thread in fabric; the needle pricks
only in a sequence of instants. We leave a mark, a furrow
in the past or the fabric traversed.

In a certain sense, we are only real when we engage with the present; there where the bow slices through the water. There is nothing before us, behind us only a furrow quickly erased.

And yet, there is memory and it still acts upon the present; and there is apprehension of the future; each one quickening or slowing depending on the case, producing a chain of events, ensuring a relative continuity.

Measure of suffering—measures of the heavens. What do they have in common? The most horrible agony, measured against the universe, is less than the tearing of a petal; infinitely less; but that contradicts what we observe. Hence the idea of the two measures. And if pain can be more profound than the universe, then joy could be more profound as well; or, rather, it cannot and should not be measured by these scales but remain apart from them—escape them, exist *elsewhere* in space. Perhaps we only suffer to the extent we are in conflict with time and space, exercised by our limits.

Then the entire world, the visible world, would be nothing but an image that does not portray us.

August

Hour when the village, from a distance, turns to
    crystal.
The sky too, at other times.
Landscape seen through the fork of a tree.
Height, expanse of the sky, its relation to the horizon,
    to the earth.

࣌

Yellow fireworks of fennel gone to seed.

࣌

Heat that nourishes, that torches, that palls.

    The world seems quite lost at times. It is impossible
to bear a comprehensive view of the world, one that
encompasses its totality, its violence, its shame. Children
are exposed, to an eye so clear, to a heart so gay.

࣌

Everything I've written, and surely what was clearest,
most serene, was written to push back the unknown, to
hold off the fear that draws near and, on certain nights,

triumphs. There is nowhere we can hide from the brush of deadly light we believe is meant to open up the future for us.

Where is the Being who will give us strength, who will grant us a moment's respite when we are almost completely caught in weariness? What is the Resurrection? The story of a dream?

That Being is farther from us than the furthest limit of the sky, more unknown than the unknown. A child has more than enough time to scream in pain before it intervenes.

How to build?

Sometimes I understand the wretched young people who sleep on the pavement in cities, who rarely feel desire and then only vaguely: Why stay upright, why procreate, why carry on in such a world? Their idleness surely accords all too well with this surrender.

Others feel rushed. Girls barely old enough to get married bare their legs and, fed with enticing images, look for someone who will free them from their floating boredom with the pleasure they desire. You see it even in the villages. Each one has her own little machine that follows her—as the hunter his dog, the fool his king— a small box from which, in a steady stream, flow the incantations of department-store sorcery, potions concocted from the dustbin's detritus. They walk, they sway their hips, smoking, slightly drunk on the radio fumes, often so lovely in bright coloured dresses, their shrewd hairstyles, so animal-like with their long tanned legs, so dumb—or so helpless that they imagine themselves to be flagships sailing past 'splendid cities'.

They're in a hurry; they paint their faces quickly like savages getting ready for battle. They go out, they close their eyes, they want their desire satisfied, they will soon be old or everything will turn to stinking ash. But whatever they do, if they only knew how quickly their colours will fade, how soon their paint and feathers will be bathed in tears. They run around, chomping at the bit, round the hive of motors, in the noise of the cement mixers, in front of houses built to fall apart quickly. What patience they'll need to pay for that race! Still, who can blame them, having seen their world? Like an anthill that an enormous stick had poked one day, just to see. The stick of Hiroshima. The cudgel of knowledge.

They run, thinking they are on their way up and out, but they are only running away. Don't ask them for the slightest effort. Their brains already can only consume pap. It would have to trickle ceaselessly into their ears as a liquid balm. Any interruption is an effort, a risk. They embalm themselves in bland treacle, soon even sugar will taste too bitter to them. Or, once they emerge from their lethargy, they'll want to be jolted, shaken. They were larvae, nymphs of insects, now they've become puppets. They're shaken or beaten. They open their mouths; maybe they'll foam at the mouth? Then they sink beneath the hammering sounds. Castalia's nymphs, dryads . . . They are nothing but dismantled insects. Blinded by the new sun, the hellish sun; struck down by its cudgel.

October

Picking a bunch of grapes one evening, I suddenly see the orb, the grape of the moon. I hold the cluster in my hand.

❧

The ideal book is not a collection of poems. It would contain poems only in its purest moments, like holidays in a year of words (the romantic episodes in *Don Quixote*?). But the ideal book is, in fact, made up of several books by various authors, each one able to realize only certain aspects, to write only certain pages.

❧

Michel Leiris' *Fibrilles*: A man who admits in all honesty that he is torn between beauty and truth. Is that because he has formed a false idea of beauty? A faithful follower of André Breton, from whom he has absorbed a number of inflections, he situates poetry in a space that is *off limits*, that is to say, in a certain sense *beyond the law*. But is this its proper place?

❧

Phaedo: false words are not only evil in themselves, but they infect the soul with evil.[14]

∂♠

Sky the colour of pale sulphur, frightening storms, out of season, as if from some infernal source.

November

Phaedo: As if it were absolutely necessary that one point remain forever doubtful, that it elude the grasp of thought, that it persist in poetic uncertainty: fleeting light.

Rereading *Phaedo*, the reasoning itself seems not at all convincing and more a masterful sleight of hand. Neither is the myth, which can seem juvenile. It is the *example* of Socrates that is most gripping and still one of the most elevated we have (whether we encounter him there, about to die, on the night of the *Symposium*, or at other moments in his life in which he embodies the spirit's smiling triumph. It is this that grips us—the example of the 'only witnesses'[15] whom, later, Blaise Pascal would believe. At the same time, the motif of the soul's *purification*, which is deemed immortal to the extent it turns towards the pure and divine, calls our attention. Here we have an original movement towards the elevated but also the seed of the Christian condemnation of the body. Eternity reserved for philosophers?

è⬤

The first snow. How the flakes melt as they near the ground, the roofs, and disappear. I think of kisses that approach the body, the skin. And of what changes and seems to disappear. Like the death of birds, of butterflies. A dissipation.

≈♣

In friendship with the forests. Why do stones, soft mosses, ivy, dead wood, mushrooms, all that makes up the soil of the underbrush, seem so *good* to us? As if we were cradled in a hand, supported and welcomed? Both bed and table?

Water trickling over rocks: as if they were opening up.

Under the trees, under the oaks' latticed screen: more than that. As absurd as it seems, the word 'friendship' comes to mind again. With the trees' blessing. Their serenity, their weightless, trembling mediation, between our heart and all-too-heavy infinity. Their porous roof brought to life by the merest wind. Under thousands of winged or floating tiles, under this filter of light, of infinity. Under those fans that winter strips down to their rough wooden handles.

By yielding to the movement of the mind in search of analogies, you let yourself be drawn towards another kind of pleasure or beauty. But then you must say once again: that wasn't it. It was the earth, the wood, the greenery, the sky; a walk, an instant's respite, a bit more innocence. It is also what seems eternal because it constantly begins anew, always the same yet without monotony. It was Time smiling like a patriarch or a mother. The immemorial. That which opposes the distraught mind. An open house. The forest is a house with all its windows and doors open. Light flows through it as through streets. It passes, enters and leaves. Light, or your dream exposed, which you will never catch hold of again?

 је

And suddenly you see yellow trees under the clouds in constant motion. A shade of yellow you don't know quite how to describe, neither lemon yellow, nor the yellow of wheat, nor that of the sun. It is somewhat pale, somewhat cold. It is the colour of certain feathers (and the entire landscape like an aviary of canaries?).

(A leaf seen up close: you observe that the yellow is a fading, a discolouration of the green that can still be seen at the base near the stem. The green retreats, flees like water, and the yellow invades the surface.)

The water glitters in the muddy furrows or resembles pieces of iron.

Elsewhere, the leaves are truly flames. The idea of *change* is very present; of an attack, a wound, and a response to that attack. Colours of the sunset (often noted already, but very fitting). A response to Time? All the forests like a setting sun, as if the year's sun were setting.

Also: last screens, last decorations before we see the frame. The earth is an empty husk. Leave us with rain under the sky's rafters. Leave us exposed but more constant.

๛

The north wind has set in, fierce, arid, cleansing. The sky is once again almost crystal clear. The chestnut trees are brusquely stripped bare. We see black crows lifted like leaves on gusts of wind: it must be a game. The tree seems to be slipping out of its leafy dress. Yet what emerges is not a nude body but a skeletal frame the colour of coal. Or rather a framework: skeletal frame makes one think of skeletons and there is nothing funereal in this scene. The framework is just as beautiful as the raiment, neither more nor less but of another kind of beauty. (Think, rather, of the wood that has not yet been consumed at the heart of a fire, especially in a dying fire.) A mast with furled sails. What is most touching about bare trees is their momentum, the way they expand upwards, the seamless transition from rough trunk to the subtle ends of the branches: the One that gracefully opens out into the Many.

(Suddenly my hands are pink. The sun rose without warning—since there were no clouds—almost hastily; the distant furnace, the hell that becomes a blessing from afar. This morning it looks to me like the mirroring heart of an invisible figure appearing in the east. Isn't there a sculpture of a man, perhaps flayed, holding his heart in his raised hand? A blessing for the fields, a scourge elsewhere.)

Another admirable aspect of a tree is that it is elegant and gnarled at the same time. It surely teaches me more about serenity, about patience, than a painting depicting a moral subject. It too is not an object but an intimate work. A marvel of countless movements, of simultaneous and successive transformations. I am groping for the connection there must be between us and these transformations. The first image that springs to mind is that of crows lifted on gusts of wind which seem to be their playthings and to escape them, to dominate and to *precede* them. Do we also *precede* in such a fashion? In the world and ahead of the world through the mind. Not just ahead of but also partly outside it, partly 'free' and *further ahead*: forerunners, often a bit troubled. The most exposed elements of a crusade always underway towards some still-undetermined point in infinity, some Orient still to be born, and on the way paying the price of what horrors? Are we able to transport ourselves in mind that far ahead, even for a moment, and conceive of this movement of worlds, which perhaps mirrors the movement in each of our souls when fascinated by inaccessible peace? Stupor. I had forgotten the measure of the worlds. But that's just it: I still sometimes believe—and I will have to adjust my analogy—that we might not only be in advance of an event, out ahead of it, but somehow also able to *elude* that which measures it. There would be the world of numbers and another world neither in it nor outside of it, displacing all images, all thoughts. We would escape through our very wounds, through the liquid of our tears. A break in measurable continuity, a tear in the fabric of matter.

In my view, you cannot definitively exclude the possibility that internal suffering is a rending of the fabric of matter.

༄

The place called the Lake has become one again. It is a marvel to see, in this dry country, the sudden wrinkling of the water in a field, and even, against the reeds of the opposite 'shore', an almost imperceptible wing of foam.

༄

The conflict between rhyme and 'truth'. At times I want rhyme in order to ensure the poem's coherence; sometimes, when it makes me say something other than what I should, I abandon rhyme, which is not satisfactory either.

༄

. . . Like the hour just before dawn, a man crossing the road in the distance seems without strength, lost. There is nothing to help him, to support him . . .

The quotidian: lighting the fire (and it doesn't start on the first try because the wood is damp. I should have stacked it outside but that would have taken time), thinking of the children's homework, of an unpaid bill, of a sick friend to visit, etc. How can poetry insert itself into all this? Either it is just decoration or it should be internalized in each of these gestures or acts: this is how Simone Weil understood religion, how Michel Deguy understands poetry, how I want to understand it. But the danger of artifice remains, of a 'dutiful', laborious sacralization. Perhaps we will be reduced to a more modest, intermediary position: poetry momentarily illuminating life, like snowfall, and still being able to recognize it. Maybe we should even consent to accepting its inherent *exceptional* character. Caught between the two, do what you can for better or worse. Or you run the risk of sectarian severity, the temptation to don the poet's frock coat and isolate yourself in 'prayer' (which is disconcerting in Rainer Maria Rilke at times). In my case, I have to accept more weakness.

ह•

Seven-thirty in the morning. The air is still. The entire world is blue, the entire world is asleep. The few grey clouds turn pink before I've finished writing their name.

Just the light shade of red, that inflammation on the edge of the mountains.

December

It is strange that, as they draw to an end, these deep, pure winter nights, in which a few stars above a yellowing horizon seem to shine brighter than at any other time of year, immediately make me think of the manger, the Magi, the biblical East. I had already been reminded of these images on a winter's evening in *Landscapes with Absent Figures*. I was drawn to them once again, yesterday or the day before, as if these images were deeper within me than I had realized and took this form because I have never been to Israel. Old, childish dreams of a gentle, deep and velvety night, illuminated with stars of silver and gold. A thin sickle of moon in the sky completes the connection and sharpens it; but perhaps it is Arabia rather than Judaea that rises in my imaginative memory (the word Arabia, its power of enchantment in Shakespeare, in Góngora). I think of the fascination an illustrated edition of the *Thousand and One Nights* held for me as a child, a fascination I experienced again in a different form but just as profoundly. It is strange that nothing in the West or in Africa ever affected me as deeply. On the contrary, my fascination seems to increase the closer I get to the East: Vienna, Prague, Bohemia, Poland, Moscow, Tibet, China (also Judaea, Persia). Why? One reason for this preference must be a form of cultural refinement found there but not here. Another is the sentiment that our origins are in the East. I can't think of anything that inspired me to dream as much as the illustrations in the Hetzel edition of Jules Verne's *Michel Strogoff*. Nothing can compare.

ॐ

At the far end of this reedy plain, Mont Ventoux appears suddenly, hovering, as if suspended by the delicate pyre, a pink pyre of trees. One drop of that light for the human hell!

ॐ

Insane asylum. The youngest appeared to have the most unhinged, the most afflicted gaze. An impression of both rigidity and instability, of rigidity 'to avoid unstability'. In a kind of sitting room on the ground floor, through a glass door with flowered curtains, you can see some madmen sitting utterly motionless, others pacing back and forth faster than necessary: a world of 'too much' and 'too little'.

It takes nothing for the narrow bridge thrown over the abyss to shudder and give way. It is not easy to face misery, distress, abasement once again in places like these. From here you return to books. You open a magazine and find scholars learnedly discussing death or language.

꒰ꔸ

A walk through C. You meet people in accord with their fate. This couple who met in a nightclub in Paris—he the accordion player, she the coat-check girl—who now enjoy eating fox in a village of three houses at the far end of a remote mountain gorge.

1967

February

In the evening, all the trees, a pink armful, ready to catch fire. In the morning, their bare branches still glisten with celestial water. They increase the light. Luminous firewood?

❧

The rain, the cries of birds, the almond tree's first blossoms: their harmony inspires joy. It is perhaps like hearing a choir sing the same thing in different voices? Or like seeing the multitude of leaves born from a single trunk? A thousand, a thousand cries, a thousand flowers, a thousand drops of sonorous water, and one single world, one single hearth?

March

Almond trees, from a distance: foam over the earth, against the dark background of earth, of ash.

From up close: green, white, yellow, that harmony so fleeting we can barely grasp it. The colour of milk.

ૐ

Plotinus on happiness: [*The wise man will tend and bear with his body for as long as possible,*] *as the musician cares for his lyre, as long as it can serve him: when the lyre fails him, he will change it, or will give up lyre and lyring, as having another craft now, one that needs no lyre, and then he will let it rest unregarded at his side while he sings on without an instrument. But it was not idly that the instrument was given him in the beginning: he has found it useful until now, many a time.*[16]

May

Irises, their pale blue, their lightness, their sky—illuminated—under the leaves, in the emergent greenery.

࢈

The planes that pass over this landscape have no connection to it, foreign thoughts, lines written in another language. They do not plough the skies. Can we say that they fly? They don't seem free. They are shot like bullets from a gun. They rend the air. Their only trace is a rumbling.

࢈

I walk. I take in the air, the expanse.
A flock of flashy jays passes.
A redstart catches fire when it leaves the tree.
The window through which distant things come.
    A porous house full of holes.
Everything has been distributed, spread out across the
    expanse.
This layer of grass and leaves on dry ground; this veil
    of day between us and the night; these shelters,
    these intermediaries. Our voice.

A double crater, a double basin: first the enclosure of oaks; further on, higher up that of the mountains. Double basin for the sky. We are in the middle. We watch space turn.

Bouquets of trees: how light and shadow mingle, opacity and transparency, movement and immobility. Thickets of wind, hives of air, sheaves of air. Attached, they move. Perhaps we are linked by death.

The earth in cracks, in scales, like a ruin. Fertile divides, in bloom. Everything rises from a central point and broadens, multiplies or scatters. Genealogical trees. Doomed, reckless seeds. Feel yourself the seed of an ancient plant whose roots are no longer visible.

Mountain on its pedestal, lifted by the light. A piece of fruit in a bowl of light. Sometimes Buddhas are carried like this. They cannot be unseated or toppled.

I remember the bridge, how moved I was on that cold day in March by the black arch of the bridge in Rust in Burgenland. A day of mother-of-pearl and birds, and those long boats, the paths to the lake between the reeds.

Screens of straw: shelter and lightness. The right measure, the right distance for the enclosure. The farmland of the Côte d'Or, its hedges and sleepy, meandering streams.

The harrow of the reeds.

ֶ℁

I still find the mountain's presence magical. Beyond the close fields and the trees seething with wind against the light, the low mountain under the almost white sky, like a piece of sky that is less bright. What is it then?

Seen from here, a dome, a flattened hump above which the sky is even brighter.

Without volume, without details, indistinct; rising above the trees, and brighter too where it touches their crowns, which gives the impression it's weightless, suspended or floating.

Colour? Barely a colour: like smoke in the air.

I had previously guessed an essential element of its magic: weightlessness. This morning, I believe I'm discovering another. Hard to define. It struck me as I turned away. It was (I'm convinced) as if there were a (friendly) presence on my left, someone (a protector?). Perhaps tied to childhood memories.

As if, as far back as I can remember, I had always had this blue presence on my left, not all heavy or hostile but sympathetic. Once more, I believe that for me it's another image of the happy *limit* which does not restrain.

Mountain——house.

&

Greedy larks.
Nightingales the colour of sand, of ash, the most
    sonorous of birds.

June

Plotinus: *Murders, death in all its guises, the reduction and sacking of cities, all must be to us just such a spectacle as the changing scenes of a play; all is but the varied incident of a plot, costume on and off, acted grief and lament. For on earth, in all the succession of life, it is not the Soul within but the Shadow outside of the authentic man, that grieves and complains and acts out the plot on this world stage which men have dotted with stages of their own constructing* (*On Providence 1, 15*).[17] As shocking as these words are, it is possible that Plotinus truly did disdain grief and death as *games* because he had a vision of Light that is still radiant today.

❧

'The flower's old age.' When the honeysuckle (or red valerian, called Spanish lilac here) wilts, we see the light frame that supported it; withered blossoms, thin mauve or grey stems, are still attached to it here and there. At the same time, little feathery wheels open up; the lower ends, tightly wound, gradually rise and unfurl. Then we see a kind of tree bearing wheels or feathered stars, ready to take flight, to swarm; silvery almost, perfect in their slenderness, even more beautiful than the flowers.

Dropping all splendour, all of its rosy hue, to make room for this filigree. Things only just attached to the stem, absolutely weightless, with only the hint of a shadow, the slightest of fertile plumages.

The honeysuckle burns for a moment, than strews its fertile, silvery ashes.

❧

Plotinus: *An eye filled with its vision, a seeing that bears its image with it; Eros taking its name, probably, from the fact that its essential being is due to this (h)orasis, this seeing (On Love, 3.5, 3).*[18]

July

Those dried grasses I noticed last year are already mixing in with the lavender, now almost blue, according to the fields. If you look quickly, you might call them white; but they are more of an ivory colour.

At first glance, the pale colour in those dark fields seems most important, and is probably a dry weightlessness audible in the word 'hay'. Although straw is too yellow. The way seeds are suspended or carried above the fields—in bells, in fans, in sacs. You can almost hear their dry sound, their crackling; they are almost diaphanous, like paper—dry air? It is moving towards whiteness, moving towards desiccation, the intangible. Screens of paper or silk, fans. Always affecting, but especially now, in the night of lavender when they leave traces of dry foam. Purification through solar fire. Also like lambs in night's violet bed. But it is motionless or only moves in place (not, as I had first imagined it, like thoughts that flit through the eye's shadow or the nocturnal dream). Seeds, bells of straw.

Butterflies flutter above it, white, rust or brown. What rises from the earth? What flies at mid-height? Butterflies all wing, practically bodiless, there only to show light, colour, between light and scents. Or scraps of coloured wind, never at rest. The most destructible, widespread, lavish thing in our world, as words are. Without heft. Once again I've gone astray round a centre that slips away but sheds light nonetheless on its detours.

≈

How shall I bear your loss, colours? And all that the sun engenders? Should I align myself with the cult of the four elements? They all nourish and purify. Where does corruption worm its way in? Who was the serpent? The tiger is pure; he is of leaping fire. Here, we are very close to the elements; that is why we love this place.

≈

Who knew to speak of the earth as the fatherland? Did the 'pagans' know? Homer, Pindar, Aeschylus?

≈

Hollyhocks, carried in the crystalline evening, after sunset, captivating. It is tempting to think of a word like incarnation, hence of flesh: blushing. Yet the connection seems so distant to me, almost dreamlike, that it must be tied to something else. Still, it's not impossible that the flower represents the dream of a pure, burning sexuality, without the burden of moods. Without stain, but real. That could, fundamentally, be it.

Openings, borne on the ends of stalks, in the crystal of evening.

Silent megaphones. Vases full of pollen. Almost translucent. As if the plant were becoming sky, or at least taking wing. Here *pink* plays an essential role. Pink flowers, women in love, lifted into the air. Titian nudes. Leda and the swan. A woman named Angelica. Raising love to these heights. A love scene suspended between heaven and earth, on a balcony.

Barely inflamed whiteness, above the horizon, in this airy glass.

Oleander: a cool blaze.

❧

At noon, above the motionless earth, a buzzard appears in the sky, hovers a long time against the wind, then crosses the celestial expanse once again, almost without beating its wings, and disappears. Round it, the sky seemed even more immense and that white immensity existed only for the bird.

August

Léon Chestov: *I believe that to represent the gods as perfect is to misunderstand them. And yet, it is necessary to understand the gods, however impossible. We must know that we do not at all know what perfection is.*[19]

September

Dreams. A less-sustained sleep reveals their number and intensity. I am struck by the distance between my dreams (to which I pay little attention in general, especially since I rarely catch hold of them) and my books. In the end, the stuff of my dreams is that of newspapers, of 'bad' newspapers. Sex and violence. Very often in the cinema's lurid form: in close-ups, obvious allegories, etc. For a time I noted the frequency of prison dreams. In my dreams, I also live through ridiculous, brutal, nerve-wracking stories of spies or gangs. Through dreams, we reconnect with common matter, the base stuff of which history is also made, today more than ever.

It is probably true that my poetry neglects these low levels too much.

Two dreams noted:

A. Beginning forgotten. It takes place in a house that is ours, yet does not resemble it. The doorbell rings. It's the new cleaning lady, whom we'd already given up on. She is lead by L. (our former cleaning lady in real life) and escorted by two dogs and two or three cats. Timidly, we protest that they might not get along with ours, although we understand it cannot be avoided. The kitchen is narrow, filled with furniture and very old utensils. Suddenly, a close-up of L.'s face with her thick, grey hair in disarray; she holds a desperately mewling kitten by the ear. I see this old, pink, wrinkled face covered with tears. She explains that the kitten is sick, doomed. (In real life we thought that of L. when we visited her recently in hospital.) We become more and more annoyed. The new cleaning lady smiles impassively.

Later, her three or four cats grab onto my legs with their claws. I cannot get them off. In a fit of rage, I chase away the woman along with her retinue.

B. A dream, large sections of which I regret having forgotten because on waking I had the sense they were of great beauty and coherence, without gaps or excess.

Only very little of the dream remains: I am walking or, rather, wandering through an enormous house that is empty and dark; empty of all furniture like an art gallery or rooms in certain *châteaux*. It seems there are two floors, each consisting of a single room, joined by a huge staircase. I am struck by the grandeur of the windows and doors. No ornamentation. An immense emptiness, dark and enclosed. I walk through it. I don't remember if I felt anxious. Perhaps. Suddenly I notice a shape that seems to be leaning against the edge of a fireplace. At first, it looks like a bundle of clothing, a kind of tweed vest (vaguely), then I quickly grasp that it is someone standing against the wall. I look only at the figure's face which, turned away, is that of a short-haired woman, probably a red-head. In any case, it is someone I don't know, someone who remains silent and who, with a movement of her arm or just through the direction in which her face is turned, gestures towards a dark door in the wall through which I am obviously meant to lead or follow her.

Then I awoke, not, as you might expect, with the feeling of having escaped a nightmare but with a sense of solemn, sovereign beauty. The door through which I was invited to pass could have opened onto death, to be sure, but also (I think this thought came to me in the dream or immediately after it) onto an alluring hell.

In connection with this, I recall that, over many years, I periodically remembered my very first (?) childhood dream about an enormous dragon of coloured wood in a mountain landscape or among clouds or in a storm. This dragon was covered with keys (as on a piano keyboard) that could have also been doors through which one could enter into its core.

October

The evening rose. The dust, the smoke of evening, pink at first, then mauve. The entire sky caught in the reflection of a distant conflagration, in this incense, dispersing into pink dust. At the end of a hot, cloudless day, in which hunters combed the hillside with whistles, blasts of horns, shouts.

At one moment, early on, near the Devès and Grangette farms, once again the earth itself and the mountain became almost transparent (to put it inadequately), mere screens before an interior illumination, below a sky that was itself only light.

And so the question occurred to me again: what is the relationship between death and the fact that we see, that we drink in this wine of light through our eyes?

A few moments later, everything, not just the sky, turned into a confusion of pink, an ashy pink shading to mauve or to blue, a slightly darkened pink, grave and tender, spare yet pervasive, like perfume.

ἐ♦

The imperceptible movement of an invisible soul and the enormous sun.

&

Morning mist, beyond the first trees. I think of John
Keats, his *Ode to Autumn*:

> *Season of mists and mellow fruitfulness . . .*

Then of Leopardi:

> *Vaghe stelle dell' Orsa, io non credea*
> *Tornare ancor per uso a contemplarvi . . .*
> (*Glimmering stars of the Great Bear,*
> *I never thought I'd be back to see you*)

If I were to place extracts from critical essays in the
'new' style (the style of almost every literary magazine
today) next to these quotes or to other examples of what
poetry has produced at its purest, would their incompat-
ibility not be obvious?

&

Poplars at night, carrying their shadow like a flag
wrapped round the pole (?). Spindles in the yellowish
evening light. Here and there, in rows or alone. What do
they say, separating themselves this way from the indis-
tinct expanse of indistinct trees? Very far away, beneath
us, as in the background of a painting? I remember two
elements at first: their form as isolated spindles, taller and
straighter than the rest, like signs or semaphores, flames,
candles; flames of foliage, flames of grass? Also that they
hold light (and shadow)—that is probably essential—
that they stand like markers in the expanse, as if each one

passed on a text with the word 'light' or the words 'evening', 'gold' and 'shadow.' They accentuate, they punctuate space, with one side golden and one side black, from a distance almost indistinguishable. Spindles upon which the shadow's silk and the day's silk are intertwined, spindles of silky shadow and gold. And once again—do not cross the boundary between true and false!—you forget the simplicity, the coolness of the trees, the air, the expanse, the hours that pass without sound. Reason that throws the truth's laws into doubt cannot counter the feeling, at once delicate and strong, that sets this boundary.

§

I have always been drawn to Petrarch's Italian, even though I don't know it well, no matter where I open his books. I *feel* this language (immediately, before any thought or analysis) as entirely distinct and porous, as if it consisted of openings filled with sound (as if one were walking through galleries of glass and open space). A resonance at once soft and crystalline. But above all, *porous*, permeated with the celestial infinity. Honeycomb. A web of words that encloses the sky or filters it as trees do?

A language suited to the Tuscan landscape; as I once believed I *saw* the verses of St John of the Cross in Majorca's landscape.

November

Autumn. Rain on fire. A landscape inflamed and frigid.
Flowers, fog, dampness. As if the rain itself were on fire.

❧

A visit to pay our respects. Under the dead woman's bed,
a dog; at the foot of the bed, three misshapen old women.
One of them rises repeatedly to sprinkle holy water on
the waxen face. In the room we must cross to reach the
deathbed, pale flowered underclothes lie upon an
unmade bed.

1968

May

Georges Bataille: *There is in nature and there subsists in man a movement which always exceeds the bounds, that can never be anything but partially reduced to order. We are generally unable to grasp it. Indeed it is by definition that which can never be grasped, but we are conscious of living in its power: the universe that bears us along answers no purpose that reason defines, and if we try to make it answer to God, all we are doing is associating irrationally the infinite excess in the presence of which our reason exists with our reason itself. But through the excess in him, that God whom we should like to shape into an intelligible concept never ceases, exceeding this concept, to exceed the limits of reason.*[20]

The sacrifice: *The external violence of the sacrifice reveals the internal violence of the creature, seen as loss of blood and ejaculations. The blood and the organs brimful of life were not what modern anatomy would see; the feeling of the men of old can only be recaptured by an inner experience, not by science.*[21]

Erotism is transgression, a rending, or it is nothing. It is the black path, the path of night. One should only speak of it if one commits oneself to it. Otherwise it is nothing but coquetry, one more fashion. Bataille's writing forces us to ask again Musil's question about the passion between Ulrich and Agathe: is there a separate morality for geniuses? A possible means of communication between the 'other state' (ecstasy) and daily life?

June

Le Thoronet Abbey. What captivated me there was the precise moment of *passage*, either from outside into the nave or from the nave into the cloister; the same captivation as with Bach's highest peaks. Ground for a proliferation of commentaries.

This space is truly an enclosure, but one that is both the most enclosed and the most open; it creates silence and allows it to blossom silently, a joyful silence, ripe as a fruit.

Compare it to the Greek temples as we now see them, through which air flows, in which the landscape, the surroundings, remain visible between the columns.

September

From a letter written by a museum curator: 'Some time ago, my colleague M. B. entrusted to me a collection of zoogenic fossils from the Burdigalian molasse basin near the village of M . . . I would like to express my heartfelt thanks for the faunistic array you have collected and especially for the eighteen samples of irregular sea urchins (of the Clypeasteroida and Echinoida orders) . . .'

If I were speaking of these same fossils, I would, following my personal requirements, describe the exact location and the very moment we had discovered them, the mown wheat field and, next to it, the field of lavender, where these discs, rounded on top and slightly hollow underneath, with their impressions of fine stitching more or less well preserved, can sometimes be found among the stones, exposed by the ploughs or the strong rains. I would try to understand why we are as touched and delighted to find them as children searching among the flotsam washed up by a turbulent sea. In other words, I search for a totality that encompasses time, life, the particular, the subjective, whereas the scientist classifies outside of lived time, he sets his categories at a remove from life.

＆

Heard the cry of a nocturnal bird that seemed unfamiliar to me. It was very close, cutting the silence, one detached note, then three tied together, shorter (its rhythm the inverse of the so-called Fate motif in Beethoven's Fifth Symphony); more cry than song, not drawn out and modulated like the tawny owl's, not as spectral, but frightening all the same. And even if I no longer search for meaning in these calls, these voices, I feel bound to the birds and to their voices in the darkness. As I was thinking this, I noticed I was filled with an irrational fear, filled with nothing but fear. And I thought again that I must try to capture such instances without any untruth, without concern for beauty or provocation.

October

Death of Jean Paulhan. One of those minds we needed
most today, for his judgement, his sense of justice.
Through his great modesty and through a necessary sly-
ness, when he seemed to be discussing minor subjects,
very specialized questions or bizarre exceptions, he was
in fact addressing what is most fundamental and most
elevated.

1969

September

Climbed up the hillside. The 'flowers on the talus deprived of dew, a pitiful sight for the traveller' (like the opening of a Gustave Roud prose piece I once knew by heart), the wildflowers along the side of the road, at eye level, blue, pink, yellow, small, and the dried grasses, white. Again they signal to me, rapidly, elusively, furtively, turning away as soon as I look at them.

Evening: stormy heat in a sky that clears little by little. The sun reappears, golden. The immobile columns of smoke over the fields give a sense of boundless peace.

Coming to rest, suspension. Hölderlin's 'golden balance'.

The relation of trees and the air.

A flock of long-tailed bushtits alights briefly in the oaks, then takes flight.

The crown of tress and sky, at my height.

ૐ

Doubt, emptiness. A wave of uncertainty. Distraction of spirit, disorder.

Contrast this to a blind wall.

᷿

Morning climb through the forest. The sun sets the branches, the damp leaves, alight. Tall grasses bend under the weight of this limpid fruit.

᷿

Montagne d'Aurouze near Saint-Étienne-en-Dévoluy, the forest of Mont de l'Enclus.

Leaving Veynes, the road rises towards la Cluse, dominated by a mountain of stone, of whitish scree, its rocky summit shrouded in haze. Deep in the broad valley, there is the same abundance of stone and little water. A kind of standing desert. Vast, but luminous talus (especially the following evening on our way back, under a clear sky), mountain of luminous scree, it rises above us almost perpendicularly, ready to collapse, arid and massive, a temple plinth, a pedestal of sand for the wildest animals, above shepherds' paths we can barely make out.

Past this, we descend towards Saint-Étienne-en-Dévoluy through a high valley, a kind of speckled plateau, spotted with piles of stone, green, yellow and white.

In the humid forest of thick moss—ferns, bilberry, raspberry bushes, wilted gentians—magically coloured mushrooms, painted bright brown, orange, pink, brilliant or pale white, like strange words on the earth's lips.

&.

The clinic in M. A little old man with a bandage much
larger than the hand it encloses, his face pale and hollow,
a tired smile, white hair—whose screams we hear when
he is with the doctor, unbearable.

&.

I raise the celestial lamp
over our brief sojourn
I wash our imperfect life
with its light
its golden justice spills over
the untidy room
the overgrown garden
the tired knees
anxiety, laughter
under its scales, higher than the mountains
the absent and the living take their place.
It illuminates my hands and wears them away.

The moon does not shine like silver, but almost. There
is silver in its lightness, glimmering in its transparency.
Above the stones that darken. When the stones turn
black, obscure, the sky decants above. Ebony and silver.

Ahead, on the sunny side, lizards, grasshoppers, the
side to which we bring our chairs and which diminishes
inexorably until the first frost.

Immobility of the air or just the silent movement of the trees.

ॐ

Walking along the mountain slope, following those meagre paths or traces, under the oaks, in the heat, reaching ancient terraces overgrown with dried grass, once again I sense the stone, the earth, unmistakable. By degrees I descend this monument that just now seems more beautiful than any man-made monument, more majestic and simpler at the same time, more satisfying, more heartening for the entire being, body and soul; offering a limpid joy with no aftertaste.

A stone sliced open, its jawbone full of crystals.

A line of white smoke mingled with the poplars follows an invisible stream in the hills' trough.

The sky's measure is still vast.

Whatever is on these slopes surprises me: a tuft of grass under trees, shadows, the pale, almost supernatural colour of the juniper bushes, suddenly this very high wall, useless, intact—and beyond it, views over the cultivated fields. The grasshoppers, like spring-loaded cases of wood, narrow and lined with red or blue. Enclosures bounded by stone over which a white butterfly silently passes, its flight jerky, jolting, mute. It gropes its way through the golden air. Its limping flight.

October

A flock of pigeons turns in the north wind and the stream
of brilliant light, above a field, beyond a line of mulberry
trees and a hedge, only slightly above the trees, revealing
now this side, now that of their wings: now a dazzling
white, now almost invisible; now shadow, now mirror
(blinding).

Something without weight or ties, half carried away,
half resolute, calligraphy on an autumn sky.

&

My table filled with dirt.

The air trembles in the trees
the wind resides lightly in the trees, it pauses there,
    lingers
and their leaves reap the sky.

The leaves tremble, shine, like so many mirrors of
    the sky.
The sky puts down its roots.

&

Despite what each person knows of hell,
from having brushed up against it or crossed it . . .

è&

At the break of dawn: the dark green of a fig tree, the
yellow of a tree farther off, stains of vines, and the mist.
Severe colours. Silence, muteness rather. You discover
a more obscure aspect of the world, of the garden. Some-
thing else disarms me, renders me speechless: these
colours and the mist before sunrise.

The world is different then, perhaps more remarkable
than at any other time. More serious, yes, more hidden,
turned inwards. The word *limbo*. Lazarus.

Would this fig tree be like Lazarus in cerements of
mist? What happens before life begins again, before
there is any noise, any direct light: of extinguished night,
of day not yet illumined. Intermediary. Purgatory. An
indirect light (still a bit spectral?). This is not truly light,
it is prior to light, prior to heat, to life.

In the doubt between night and day
surrounded by mist that lingers like something not
    yet born
before there is any sound
how deep and severe it is, the fig tree's green, how
    silent the yellow of distant leaves
surprised in their tree-life like strangers, guardians,

181

in a light that is not light, an illumination preceding
    life.
and in such silence that the leaves' green seems darker,
    the yellow more unfamiliar.
Tree of limbo! Still without shade to offer a hesitant
    soul orientation or rest.

Surprised before dawn, the fig tree is of such solemn
    green and farther off that mass of yellow leaves,
which appeared in the mist before dawn, before any
    sound,
tree of limbo! still without shade or trembling or
    murmurs
for the repose or orientation of the soul that no longer
    knows.
Tree hung only with blackened, empty purses,
tree with nothing but large, immobile leaves as dark as
    the bronze of a mute gong,
or stifled by mist.

ঽ▲

Hölderlin before Antiquity. It seems our situation is not
favourable (overburdened with culture), *but* one must
understand one's 'formative disposition' to avoid being
led astray or returning to ancient ways.

ঽ▲

Afternoon. Under a grey or more often blue-black, soot-coloured sky, the intensity of the light greens, the yellow of the vines or the reeds, the shades of rust or purple stealing over the orchards: never have I seen such richness kindled by black, flames, sparks all around. Not a celebration as in June, but something more solemn, more 'internalized' (as if space were a room?), an opulence, a richness on a dark background that is not the night; thick, opaque, brown—or the clouds of soot, of ominous ink. A military celebration, a conqueror's glory.

This is also the time when the earth reappears almost everywhere, wood and earth; the very beautiful moment of earth, of soot, crossed by two pigeons whiter than milk.

ટ♣

Gospel. It begins like a fairy tale, with the Three Wise Men, astrologists who crossed the desert, carrying gold and myrrh as if for a courtesan; with the angels who enter destitute houses or who sing from the four corners of the heavens; with the night and the smell of the stable and the star that sometimes resembles brightly shining straw. The fear and threats of the masters, the trembling of a few old men who hope, and all this disruption round a *child* (a child the Greeks more or less ignored).

In Hölderlin's 'vision-filled desert', there is a fakir dressed in rags, with only grasshoppers to eat, who makes prophecies.

The first of Christ's words that are related to us, in the Gospel of Saint Luke, I believe, is his rather brutal answer to his bewildered parents: 'Why were you searching for me? Did you not know I must be about my Father's business?'

Then it is back to the desert, the angels and the wild animals, and the 'temptation': to be nothing more than another magician or an earthly king.

❧

A Julien Green interview on the radio. A man with perfect manners—better manners, certainly, than RK, who constantly interrupts him—a chivalry that seems almost outmoded and a sense of humour as refined as the rest of him. The clarity and assuredness of his language is striking even in the most cursory readings of his *Journal*. It gives you the feeling of welcoming into your home a man who is the very best company, who never puts himself forward, a man whose soul is of the highest quality.

With Stanislas Fumet he performed a rather comical duet deploring the Church's progressivism. You'd think they were two elderly English ladies scandalized by a divorce in the royal family. It's not that I don't understand or share their sentiment from some remove. But I can measure the extent of my remove when they evoke truths established by Thomas of Aquinas, truths Fumet calls, I believe, the 'doctrinal deposit of faith', which they don't want anyone to touch. Green says softly, 'I believe I am once again speaking like a fanatic . . .' after having declared that, after all, it was not a bad thing for the Church to be rid of doubters. I realized then that I find this form of belief not only foreign but also incomprehensible.

&

Rilke's 'angels' were probably not by his side in his death throes. Christ might have been, since he gives the meaning to death that Rilke demands. It seems that we do not wish for the same angels to live as to die.

&

Snow. The snow here does not fly, nor does it fall. It seems, instead, to rise. This brings joy to childhood. Like the clouds of gnats that disperse in the summer wind.

1970

January

Inside and outside. I think again of those occasionally embarrassing questions students in Geneva or Neuchâtel have asked me (embarrassing not because they are indiscreet or hostile but because they are so subtle). For example: 'So you believe that we create only what already exists?' My inability to answer such questions bothers me. Yet I'm reassured by the answers Borges, that most subtle of writers, gave when Georges Charbonnier asked him to define literature. Borges did not know what to say at the time other than that he experienced poetry as a physical shock, an emotion. A bit further on, there is also this phrase: 'Writing is to some extent the opposite of thinking . . .' As if there were, in fact, two authors, the real one and the one constructed by readers and critics. And today critics are ever-less-willing to recognize the real one while the authors themselves begin writing 'outside-in'.

Translation. In Nestor Ibarra's book on Borges, the author (Borges' translator into French) criticizes his colleagues, especially Roger Caillois, whose version he finds too timid. But I wonder if Ibarra's version, with his worry about anything getting lost, does not betray

Borges (about whom he writes very well) more than Caillois' more timid version. Ibarra, no doubt a Spaniard, doesn't understand French as we do. I also wonder if the poems are as good as he claims, and if Borges' prose is not much superior.

February

My hands, frog feet. That same sense of delicate bones
when you snap frogs' legs.

❧

Sweat. Recover its meaning. Mortal secretion, unclear
water, a surging up of what is underneath. Unhealthy.
Like death on one's skin? A veil, a vicious fog. Sweat of
the coward, of the obese, of the feverish. Sweat and sen-
sual are connected, not just through assonance. As a kind
of improvised defence.

❧

Old man, frailer, more tremulous than the first
    shadows of the year,
old worn-out doll no one will repair again
soon good only to be discarded
already unloved

touched by February's warm, raw light
by untamed February

cold sweat of fear
when spring is like the sweat of the earth.

188

1971

April

The lesson of several courses I taught on Rilke, then on five French Swiss poets: an alignment in my approbations or reservations that surprises me most of all, as if I still had trouble believing that I am truly *one* person with my own choices, rejections, leanings. In the end, all this effort reassures me that, in the quite disparate works I've studied, the moments that are 'truest', most 'pure', are achieved when the writer has 'honed in on his own centre', shed all mythology, whether traditional or of his own invention: Rilke *after* the *Duino Elegies*, Charles-Ferdinand Ramuz without 'the bread and the wine' and all that goes with it, Maurice Chappaz without the Valais 'brother of India', Pierre-Louis Matthey and Edmond-Henri Crisinel reduced to their intimate biographies, Gustave Roud—and it was in his case that this aspect appeared most clearly to me—after he finally allowed elements that were entirely particular to his life to enter into his poetry: the house in Carrouge and the house where he was born, his garden, or the old horn used to call the footmen for dinner, instead of the more or less typical, if not symbolic, plough or scythe, and the peasant like a statue of a pagan god.

ও

The salutary example of Samuel Taylor Coleridge's notes. Now that is how it should be done. But is it possible, was it possible?

May

By dint of specifying where poetry is, never being able to grasp it again?

❧

Another lesson of these same courses: the impossibility of returning to the past (Ramuz's archaism, abandoned at the end of his life), the impossibility of maintaining 'classical' rigour (Pierre-Louis Matthey's *Alcyonée*). They both ring false.

❧

Reading Marcel Granet on Chinese as a language of *symbols*, not well suited to abstract thought, but on the other hand one especially apt in conveying what is perceptible and particular. It is said that, in the West, poetry is what we have that is most Chinese. The English: said to be the most practical and most definite of people, do they not also have the most elevated lyrical poetry?

❧

In Granet's *La Pensée chinoise*, a passage on the festival celebrating the end of winter: '. . . *there was most often a greasy pole trial. The pole was erected in the centre of the House of Man, which was the prototype of the* Ming t'ang *and was an underground house, because, once you had climbed to the top of the pole, you could suckle the sky— that is how one becomes* Son of the Sky—*or rather suckle the celestial Bell, but the teats of the "celestial Bell" (these are stalactites) are suspended from the ceilings of caves. By mastering the climbing trial, the new* Son of the Sky *earned the right to add his line to the* gnomon, *his hash to the* cylinder: *he was henceforth identified with the* Royal Way.'

For the Chinese, opposites are less contraries than *complementary* contrasts and change in meaning according to their 'headings'.

In a later passage: '. . . *true death, on the other hand, entailed the sealing of all the body's orifices. The deceased's eyes were closed, as was his mouth. From antiquity on, no doubt, all openings were sealed with jade: this custom is related to the one requiring that the Seven Stars of the Great Bear be drawn on coffins.*'

The simultaneous sense of the concrete (the disdain of abstraction) and of ritual (senseless precision of etiquette). This corresponds to the profound movement of poetry: the concrete, ritual, order, the *cosmos*.

❧

My present wish is to be able to write in prose and as a writer of prose. I know this is unfeasible. What to do?

The temptation of thought increases accordingly. To extend the questions my books have asked towards what I have so often affirmed: that one should avoid thought as much as possible?

In me, the sense of the unknown frustrates a certain rationalism. I don't believe in miracles; but in mystery, perhaps.

Almost immediately, one is driven to juggling with words.

I would like to confine myself to the particular, the intimate, to what is experienced intimately. At the same time, it seems absolutely impossible to speak of beings one is close to as long as they are living or close, unless one is willing to be more immodest than I am able to be. How can a novelist who finds his subject matter in his own life live his daily life knowing that everything he experiences will be material in a book? A madness that would be best reserved to the solitary writer.

Therein lies the risk, for me, of shying away into the general or into 'absent figures'.

On the other hand, my complete inability to 'invent' a story.

❦

Hölderlin with the carpenter Zimmer: 'Nothing else will happen to me . . .'

❧

The river flanks the hillside then drops farther on in a small waterfall, filled with algae, long blades of grass, yellow irises. Beneath the trees. Its slow and silent movement. It has crossed high meadows where willows and aspen grow. Its water appears dark.

❧

To burn, in spirit, all these books, all these words—all these innumerable, subtle, profound, mortal thoughts. To open oneself up to the falling rain, swarming with gnats, insects, to this country of grey and green; to the various species of trees, of green; to a creaking in the stone wall or wooden door.

May

Iris. *The great iris orchards of maladies.* Did I really write or read this verse in the past? I remember having associated these flowers with more or less murky desires long ago: foolishness, literature.

The scent of irises, more than any other flower's, takes me right back to my childhood as if it were spent among them, near them.

They bloom here under the fig tree, against a background of unevenly shaded greenery. They blossom like openings between clouds, like clear sky, like distance, like the coolness of a wellspring. Perhaps that can be said of all blue flowers, but irises have a particularly airy quality. They are like suspended pavilions (Chinese), raised above the ground on their stems, at once open and sheltered, a kind of crow's-nest or lighthouse lantern, a circular balcony. But do not look at them for too long: you see them best in passing, preoccupied with other worries, other tasks, other paths.

I write in the glow of these blue lanterns, so fragile once they have emerged from their silken buds.

Irises, companions. Opening doors, locks?

Irises, weightless blue keys.

Celestial keys.

Empiricism and theory. My natural tendency is to be suspicious of theories, therefore to proceed from small facts, from the bottom, from the centre one inevitably forms for oneself. Better to behave well within one's limits and without theory, than to behave badly with a theory of the good. That is what I try to do. Devoid of any political or religious faith, one can strive to act according to a discreet fraternity, relative but real. One can behave as if one did not necessarily judge others inferior to oneself and so on.

Nevertheless, in some respects this is a facile solution and certain situations can show it to be entirely insufficient. In war, for example, or in a revolution. When one is forced to take part. But can one take part if one lacks any deep conviction? How can one determine which is the lesser evil? It seems that every solution is simply a lesser evil.

I think my reflections, as a whole, would lead almost inevitably to Musil's sad scepticism. For him, all progress was made at the cost of some regression. Is it all, then, in vain? This conclusion also seems untenable.

We need more than 'socialism with a human face' (which itself seems nearly impossible), we need a socialism that is not materialist, rationalist, scientific. We need a socialism that can recognize the role of the unknown— as when we leave a place at the table for the unexpected guest. That would prevent reducing men to numbers, even if great efforts are made to ensure that all calculations are made as equitably as possible.

Perhaps that which is most scandalous about the human condition is precisely what requires us to maintain our conception of the unknown—within which this scandal would become meaningful. The more we want the gods to be reasonable, the more scandalous these scandals are. Would a god—good or cruel—not know how to be a god? Would Christ have died simply so as to make the scandal more shocking?

The human condition is a scandal that can inspire horror or despair. However, we see that no one could have restricted themselves to the early stirrings of revolt. No explanation can calm them. Unless the worst is simply a sign of the better?

Even if you cannot embrace any political doctrine for lack of faith, you can still defend the 'lesser evil'—develop it, make it liveable. It's not much. It's understandable that young men—generous and energetic—demand more.

è∙

The old cat died this morning. The first one we ever had, found by chance, who was dearer to us than many others. Yesterday afternoon, a grey cat suffered convulsions by our door. This morning it was her turn; because she was lying on stone, her mouth kept hitting it hard and became more and more bloodied. Poison probably.

The neighbour came to finish her off, with two blows of his spade.

≥●

Poetry. The better you understand how it should be done, the less you are able to write it. Virtuosity comes with the void.

≥●

One more lesson from my courses: the recourse exclusively to subjectivity, in Rilke, leads to a dead-end; and the recourse to elements outside of pure subjectivity, in Ramuz, in Chappaz, is in part artificial, forced.

Pure subjectivity can lead to mannerism, narcissism, idolatry: art as the ultimate religion. For example, Rilke admired Cézanne for missing his mother's funeral in order to paint. Kassner found his admiration disgraceful. Thus, Rilkean subjectivity has a more authentic ring than the mythology Ramuz tried to resuscitate through the peasant world.

≥●

The temptation to understand, to know: it grips you again, constantly, out of vexation from having to settle for almost nothing. However, almost as soon as it recurs, it becomes clear that it is endless, or leads nowhere. Unless this is due to pure incapacity on my part?

≈

Christ does not seem to have had a real, tangible, presence to me, not during my religious instruction. At that time, I now think, the divine mostly represented an invisible authority, a moral order, something like a higher conscience that made you hesitate to commit this or that sin, especially, of course, the carnal ones. It was not just a negative, menacing, constraining power but a severe exigency playing a role that was certainly not useless or only unhealthy. All in all, I don't think I am changing things in hindsight. Our instruction then was essentially a *moral* one, in accordance with the Protestant spirit. Our ministers were certainly not visionaries.

Perhaps through Bach's *Passions*, which I discovered and listened to passionately at the time, Christ did take on a greater dimension, a stronger presence, at least for as long as the *Passions* lasted. Nevertheless, I believe I can claim that he did not once enter my most inner self for any length of time. Not that godlessness, on the other hand, was ever a creed for me.

≈

I generally found the ministers' tone unbearable. I still do. Whether they maintain the traditional unctuous tone in a clumsy effort to create the remove Latin so perfectly does elsewhere, or whether they adapt the modern, direct tone, possibly even more out of place than the former. The churches were cold and filled with old women dressed in black. Later, in Paris, I preferred the priests mumbling in the back of a chapel, where candles burned at all hours of the day. Their very strangeness made them seem closer to God. They seemed to be members of a secret society dispersed throughout the world and always under threat of persecution. (I remember that once I lingered in the church of Saint-Sulpice as in a refuge. I did not imagine then that I might have encountered Jacques Audiberti there. Old and unwell, Audiberti found in Saint-Sulpice, as he writes in *Sunday Awaits Me*, a 'thermal balloon of charitable coolness'.) The pastor was for us just one more 'regent' (that is what we called the teachers in our villages).

Today, their task has become so difficult that some will go to any lengths to fulfil it, but they degrade it. They no longer speak using the Unknown as a foundation but use the terms Supreme Good or Justice with almost no sense of sacredness.

Do I have any 'thought' on this that I can put into words? At the most I have an assumption that there might be (here I need a plu-conditional verb tense, a hyper-interrogative form) somewhere, nowhere—beyond all distinctions—something, nothing—beyond opposites—like an all-encompassing light in which the worst would be explained, would no longer need an explanation, without our understanding in the slightest what had happened or how. A light in which all elements of reality would play unequal parts; and these parts would be more restricted the more complex, fragile, vulnerable, ambiguous their constitution. Certain men, having seen this light from up close, would devote themselves to spreading it, each in his own language and with the means available to him in his particular place and time. Occasionally to the point of fanaticism and martyrdom.

Christ would have been one of the men whose radiance was more contagious than others, showing a way, an opening, through the acceptance—not the elimination—of rending, of suffering. But these messengers would themselves be subject to the laws of time and their radiance would at length weaken, grow dim. Now almost no reflections of this light remain. The memory of a reflection, infinitely dispersed, shattered.

Without our being able to understand why.

Or is it rather, as some have claimed, that this light was merely a veil covering absolute darkness and that truth is, in fact, the absolute dark? If that were the case, our existence and the world's would be even more mysterious.

ॐ

According to Leopardi, man's illusions and greatness are inseparable. In classical poetry, it is nature that speaks; in modern poetry (the one we call Romantic), it's the poet. For Leopardi, this is evidence of disastrous ageing.

ॐ

Illusions, errors, approximations (religions) that still designate a right path. Figures that have guided us, that distanced themselves from us or that we rejected.

A crowd led astray, dispersed, all now without companions but aware that they had once had them. The young kill their father only to substitute another for him; they cannot manage without guidance.

What does the gods' disappearance signify? We cannot, in any case, claim that it's a reason for celebration, that it's deliverance (or not yet?). It seems, rather, an occasion for mourning.

And so, in these depths, in this ending, this destitution, this incapacity: a great distancing. In homage, I am sent books I do not understand or, half-understood, drop from my hands. I, with my trees, my flowers, not ignorant enough to be a naïf, too ignorant to join the ranks of the learned, the linguists, with my fears, my cowardice, my small portion of life, of blood, of words. Worried about some sad, horrible or hopeless thing that might animate and darken my words—and not some study of them—with the paralysing debate between that which makes of these words a true movement and that which tends to falsify them, because, in the meantime, they have become for me too a living and a chance for success. I, with the same old worn-out questions, perhaps taking more steps backwards than forwards and a voice that is not growing any firmer—dreaming of combining the lightness of things with the weight of time, of making 'something' of this combination—someone in the distance who watches his solitude grow, his age, his weakness, his fear—and at the same time birds fly over a garden, the wind blows, you understand nothing or are afraid of understanding too much. And yet, the sky endures, remains. I write exactly as I have said one should not write. I am not able to grasp the particular, the private—the exact details escape me, slip away; unless it is I who shies away from them.

꙳

Irises, lifted high on their stems, bright—above the leaves, the ground, raised like spheres, balloons ready to fly away.

꙳

The flies' buzzing. Measured tolling of a bell for the dead in the vaguely white summer sky. Let us pray for our sister Marie-Louise Boudon.

August

A friend's house in T., between Dieulefit and Bordeaux. Hardly more than thirty kilometres from here, to the north, landscape of the Alpine foothills, with cowbells, cool evenings, very large trees, beautiful terraced meadows held in place by high walls of dark, heavy, irregular stone blocks. Ferns, streams, tall grasses. Leaving the farm at night, the umbels, clustered in groups, look almost like lights. The ancient owner, a small, toothless man in his eighties who appears younger, wearing a frayed and dirty canvas hat with a wide, twisted brim, his face calm and almost childlike, says without bitterness things full of wisdom in fine, discerning language (the goats, he says, are 'petty'). Meanwhile, his daughter stands on the cart, mute, her head slightly tilted to one side, a funny smile on her lips, probably a little 'slow'. She says to AM: 'I haven't grown up . . .' She is probably forty, even fifty.

September

Saint-Aubin. Herds of cows you can't see (behind a field of tall corn or dip in the landscape or a hedge), but you can hear their bells: as if a church were moving round the fields.

You see them seek out the shade of the orchards, settling themselves down heavily, spread out like yellow boulders. The peacefulness of their movements, their languor, towards the shade or towards the trough.

The smell of a pigsty, suffocatingly acrid.

This sloping orchard in late afternoon, the grass under the trees is already dark, and the trees, at least some of them, still lit by the sun, golden. What was it in this view that led me to ask once again a question with no answer?

❧

Have I so perfectly grasped certain fugitive thoughts that I am justified in abandoning the effort to better translate them? Or is it that they can 'express themselves' but cannot 'be expressed', that they must clear a path through me and not be grasped?

Giuseppe Verdi's immense *Requiem*, Carlo Gesualdo's calls and sighs, the conclusion of *Das Lied von der Erde*. You think again of the immense symphonies that Gustav Mahler carried within himself. You envy him such magnitude when you yourself can barely manage a few notes in the margins.

❧

Whoever climbs a hill in search of purer thought risks, in the long run, finding only the void and may perhaps even turn against purity out of sheer exasperation. Better to get lost in less elevated regions.

❧

Burial. Never had a priest made me think of an illusionist until today. Perhaps because he performs here, in this chapel, in front of a purple curtain behind which he and the altar boy disappear after each 'number'. Perhaps even more because of the kind of black box he sets on the altar at the beginning of the ceremony. The altar boy, the most cheerful, most mischievous, boy in the village, with his feigned gravity through which a smile or even laughter often flickers, is himself the most convincing response to death. And yet, there is the story of Emmaus—its strangeness prevails over worn-out rites. And the last scraps of Latin.

The coffin is like a boat one blesses before its launch on a long voyage, the aspergillum is like a phallus. There are several marvellous moments in the liturgy, 'may the choirs of angels receive her' and does this passage not end with Lazarus? '. . . and with Lazarus, who was once poor, may she find eternal rest.'

❧

In a letter from Cézanne to Victor Chocquet, 11 May 1886, Gardanne: 'The sky, the boundless things of nature always attract me and offer me the chance to look with pleasure.' You'd think it was a sentence from Hölderlin grown old.

❧

Leaves of corn in the wind, banners, Tibetan prayer flags.

Meadows and sheep. A circle of sheep on the shore of the Berre (beyond it, reeds, a neglected orchard of peach trees) and, more silent, more supernatural behind the Morin farm, already in the shade, behind the tall grasses, two black dogs run through vast swathes of very green grass.

Past the large ploughed fields, the earth turned over, massive.

❧

Winter is perforated.

The vegetation is a net with ever-larger mesh, an ever-more-porous filter. 'Things are now becoming clearer', that screen, that protection is now less necessary. It is as if we were rising. The sky triumphs even as it grows pale.

Quick, children, play
beneath the leaves, in the spell of sunshine:
the light is in the garden.
(As if it had stopped there to visit, or to wander there
strolling, playing.)
You would have passed through there, seen the trem-
    bling shadows . . . (The last flowers and the sphere
    suspended in the dark, boundless space . . .)
Children, candle flames, who holds you?
Voices, words, and the wind.

October

Six o'clock in the evening. The moon is light, almost translucent. The trees all around are absolutely motionless, almost strange. The weather is mild, the mountains painted with a light precision, a large fire of leaves, black and red, in a garden, its smoke rises towards the chestnut trees' slower fire. A flock of birds flies in a straight line. Rarely do we experience clearer, milder moments.

In this peaceful setting, the flames seem of a different nature, they dig a hole . . . Hectic, crackling, frenzied.

෴

Knee uncovered by sleep, fog, calls of owls, as if they were lost.

෴

In 1899, Chestov wrote that Alexander Pushkin was one of the first to answer the essential question: 'How can the poet preserve the most sublime part of his soul?' And he cites these lines of Pushkin's:

All, all that threatens to destroy
Fills mortal hearts with secret joy

Beyond our power to explain—
Perhaps it bodes eternal life![22]

❧

Friedrich Nietzsche: *Not to be a Soldier of Culture without
Necessity. . . . first do superior actions and secondly seek the
superior wherever and under whatever names it is to be
found; . . . Only he who can do nothing better should attack
the world's evils as the soldier of culture.*[23]

❧

Not fog, but a grey mist, like the down that covers cer-
tain fruits, in the evening, over the fields, and the sun
purple and round in this grey.

The wellspring in the forest. Under a cover of pines,
its face of moss-covered, hunchback rocks, its mouth at
ground level, black, always dry; except this spring, after
the snow and the long rain-showers, flowing or, rather,
dripping, resonant with drops, refreshed with drops—
like bells, ringing tears, cool, inexplicably joyful.

Greyness, isolated birds calling in the trees turning
to yellow, brown, rust. The colour yellow and the cold.

November

High, dark slopes, feathered or dusted with snow.

Fire of leaves, the leaves themselves are cold flames.

Beneath the rolls, the supple columns of smoke, you wait for the flames to bloom round the ashes' tattered edges. Like foxes, they run over the ashes' snow.

Hanging from dead branches like flags from their poles, obeying the wind, shaken, exalted by the wind. Short-lived flags, soon torn, stretch aggressively, rising, fraying. They recall the shapes of mountains. Burning, ephemeral mountains, frightened and frightening. Flickering tongues. Angry cries.

Transparent too almost insubstantial, without any thickness, like transformed air, in the grip of some mystical delirium.

Gripping their prey, which almost immediately turns to ash, shattered, scattered, weightless. Making their victims lighter. *It's Venus wholly fastened on her prey . . .*

Born of debris, of worn-out things, used up, fallen.

Meanwhile, the high, white, radiant clouds roll through the sky like foam-covered waves.

I can almost see the earth, the garden through the smoke, through the inflammation, this crazed ramp, this trembling barrier, this tearing away from the ground. The smoke subsides as it rises in slow billows.

(I think of the children who have abandoned themselves to it. I wouldn't even put my hand in . . .)

The smoke, like blue milk, like yarn spun from shadows.

એ

The snow on Mont Ventoux, far off, in the evening when the sky turns dark blue, grey, almost black, and the entire landscape also darkens: brown, green, black—that distant stain is like a lighted lamp, no, not a lamp (again, I come up against the inexpressible), a radiance, something poignant, as when a bird reveals the luminous underside of its wings in mid-flight, lit up like a mirror hit by a ray of the sun or, rather, of the moon because of its pallor? This lunar reflection—surrounded by dark blue earth and sky, steel blue, raven blue, storm blue, this darkening that shows in its heart this bit of snow.

1972

February

Leopardi, *Zibaldone* (June, 1820): . . . *A nation of philosophers would be the most narrow-minded and cowardly in the world. That is why our regeneration depends upon something we might call a super-philosophy which, in its comprehension of the totality as well as the most minute aspects of things, could bring us closer to nature. This should be the accomplishment of our age's extraordinary thinkers.*

On the fact that when nations disappear, when differences are erased, man has fewer and fewer common interests and becomes ever-more egotistical: *all alike and all divided*, whereas before they had been *all unlike and all united*.

Man lives only by religion or illusion. This proposition is as accurate as it is irrefutable: if religion and illusions were completely eradicated, supposing that were possible, all men and even children once they reached the age of reason (as children essentially live on illusions) would kill themselves without fail . . .

❧

Dream. On the Trans-Siberian railroad, crossing endless, grey, foggy plains by night and thinking about what Siberia means (a word like the lash of a whip, a gust of icy wind, because of what we know about it), thinking about the camps, about Osip Mandelstam. I'm with a young woman I don't know who will accompany me as far as China. I hear her weeping quietly. She says she doesn't know why. She protests when I ask if I am to blame, I who am too old for her and who has made her into a sort of prisoner. She seems sincere. And so, since she is standing up against the window, I open her blouse as if I wanted to show the beauty of her face and breasts to the moon illuminating a landscape of forests and snow with its diffuse light. And I ask her urgently why such beauty was given to her, why it exists, why it is given to me, too? Her face gradually brightens. And yet we did not find an answer.

❧

The River Lez, swiftly flowing, the colour of mud, of earth, like a field in motion, tilled water. Fog nearby. The sound of water in the fog.

Higher up, on the wooded slope at the river's edge, a large fox several steps from us, almost orange and white, runs away.

March

Victor Hugo in *The End of Satan*: 'The shape of his
shadow pleases the fields.'

In *The Angel Liberty*:

*Suddenly, in a formless corner of the heavens
She saw the vast stable of the clouds.*

Peach trees. Pêchers. Some might be tempted by its
homonym, *péché*, sin. No. There is no connection. Mar-
vellous orchards in winter, violet, that violet wood, those
violet cages, that mesh at half-height. It is the colour that
arrests the eye and stirs it. Surely this is not only because
it is rare, unique among the species of trees in the region.
But due to something more secret still. The colour of twi-
light, just before nightfall? I am groping. Warmer, more
sumptuous than the other orchards, so beautiful as well.
Always in harmony with and connected to the bare earth.
There is the bare earth, the bare trees (but not dead—on
the contrary, filled with the slumber of their sap): a reserve
of flowers and fruit, a sheath for flowers, a frame for
nature's fireworks. And there is also its multiplicity, its
'regulation' as orchard: a kind of suspended trap, of
tracery. These are elements common to all orchards in
winter. With peach trees, there is also their strange purple
colour.

Not blood red. Between fire and the night (violet is a blend of red and blue), not between fire and ash. Fire that is not attenuated, not exasperated, but deepened, ennobled (?), enriched. And yet it is not fire: there is no agitation, no violence. A colour. Supported on brown pillars.

When in bloom, like the ones I am looking at now, lost in the gardens, against the light, against a background of early grass, what are they? The only colour amongst the greenery, the mists, the shadows, the grey of the road that glimmers at intervals in the distance. A colour that can only be called pink. Something luminous, a revelation of light. Perforated by shade: generous, divided, murmuring or humming.

Like a cloud lost in a garden (and clouds are, in fact, this same colour: white or pink), therefore as a different element, lighter, celestial. A combination of fire and air? It is suspended there like fortunate dust, like an anticloud, rather, a hole in the terrestrial sky, in the grassy sky?

Peach trees: dawn suddenly caught in their branches. (The flamingos, in the sand.)

❧

The flights of pigeons round the farms, their mirrors. In spring: the sky's blossoming.

≥●

Eight o'clock. Shadows marching through the garden and the sun's haze, leaving a trail of their breath's light smoke. The grass should be wet, the earth heavy; the air is still cool. Clumsy shadows in the morning's golden haze.

April

The trees' useless balm.
(Sometimes I loathe it, as now and then I loathe all
    poetic balm.
This one, in any case, is unbearable unless it is of an
    unusually high quality, which is extremely rare.
One ends up condemning oneself; but perhaps also
    taking a step forward or allowing, assisting it?)

May

Those whom the sun is not able to warm, walk through
    summer like frail bundles of bones.
A rattling cage of bones holding almost no fire.
Fire breathes in the lantern of bones.

❧

Gottfried Benn. It is curious to see, in the uneven French
translation, how Benn moved from a funereal expres-
sionism, through a kind of cubism (the Tower of Babel
of places, languages, worlds), to that rigorous form that
affirms the 'soldier's honour' and strives to oppose the
void with a form that, despite it all, is harmonious and
superior. But was that the right way?

    I am perhaps too docile in following my inclination
when I find here too greater truth in more 'simplicity'—
between the extremes of frenzy and this constrained
'classicism'. That is to say, to a certain extent, in verse
that allows room for that old complaint or that ancient
wonder. In Benn's poem for the Danish woman, for
example, which recalls the Montale of *Dora Markus*, or
in that other one, in which he comes upon a postcard his
mother had sent him from Jena, or in one of his fullest
poems—his 'Ode to Autumn', *September*:

    You, bending over the fence with phlox . . .

୨ଈ

History, *evolution*. If we consider them methodically, rationally, making a great effort to understand them, perhaps our conclusions will be despairing. For the past one hundred years, almost all prophetic voices—whether they are voluntarily so or not—speak of the *end*. (In Benn, again, how many 'last' gestures or 'last' words . . .) A motion towards ruination or a fall: Leopardi, Baudelaire, but also Trakl. The sense, almost the certainty of imminent death.

Nevertheless, if it is true that a 'black spot', a final opacity, resists every one of our attempts to understand anything whatsoever, we could assume that it is precisely through this black spot that something like an insane illumination might pass, that a hope (but this word is too light) might seep in.

But I need to specify that this thought must not be understood as an axiom from which the world might be more or less easily rebuilt. It is essentially obscure, evasive, good only, one could say, to keep us from losing our footing, to help us breathe in the worst circumstances which will nonetheless not improve. An aide, certainly, but one that can be neither demonstrated nor defined.

An encouragement to remain outside of systems that presuppose a historical movement upwards or downwards.

220

Trees and birds. When we see a tree from above or when one grows next to a window we can lean out of, we understand better that trees are for birds or, simply, that's when we notice it. Trees are their domain, their open cages, their swings, their ladders. A kind of pavilion with many floors or a tower with flexible springboards—lit up, if it is an acacia tree, with white lanterns of cheap paper that will soon be crumpled.

Pleasure and the vague emotion associated with the word 'pavilion' are not unrelated to this. Living in trees means living in an unconfined, porous space, open to the breezes and near the plant world. The Chinese gardens in which poets composed their subtle paeans of the world.

❧

Remnants of a dream. My mother and another old woman, her youngest sister, perhaps, at home, sitting at the table. I am struck by the sadness in their closed faces. She talks about my father and some business he was caught up in involving some shady character about whom he knew the truth. At that point, my father enters with a guest, a well-groomed man in the prime of life despite his head of completely white hair. My father scolds because the salad is not ready. At a certain point, the guest jostling me in passing. Those are the only parts

I can remember, but, once again, I'm surprised and struck by the hard, dark aspects of this hopeless dream and the uniformly sinister tone in these apparently insignificant scenes or fragments of scenes. I also remember that the visitor was probably the shady character my mother had mentioned initially.

When I woke up at four or five in the morning and faintly heard the nightingales' singing and the more plaintive cries of some nocturnal bird (I have yet to figure out which species), old age appeared to me, unavoidably, in all its implacable harshness, and I kept telling myself that with one's eyes open to all the horrors in the world, no existence is bearable, unless one's faith borders on insanity. Night thoughts that light helps dissipate. And in the morning, there was the rain crossed by the birds.

ક

Dream. It seemed to me that I had never seen more beautiful countryside in my life. It must have been in the south of the Massif Central (in my dream I remembered having already passed through there) in a twilight you might find in paintings by Nicolas Poussin and most certainly can be seen in some of Balthus': mountains of lava, of basalt, shades of black or violet, dominating vast slopes covered with dark forests that stretched to the horizon; and elsewhere (behind me?), a pink or purple light. Its sheer beauty brought tears to my eyes. Especially when

I noticed, stretching out below me as I stood on one of the slopes that descended towards infinity under a golden light, a long river valley, a wheat-coloured enclave surrounded by the forests' darkness. I don't know why it inspired as much exaltation in me as a vision of paradise. But my emotion, my jubilation, was to grow even greater when I noticed in the foreground, very near, thin streams gushing white water, some of which followed the hillside horizontally like the 'bisses' in Valais, others dropped straight downwards. An old shepherdess was sitting on the edge of the highest stream that flowed parallel to the road. All I could see of her were her hands, roughened from work.

When I had to tear myself away from this place and find a hotel, I realized I was much farther from home than I had thought and returning would be problematic.

June

Dream. Shut up in a house, more precisely, in a brothel. It begins with a pleasant curiosity in scenes glimpsed briefly and which my memory does not seem to have dared retain. The atmosphere is spoiled by the vile, insistent menace of an elderly gent with a businessman's face (like the factory manager in *Modern Times*). The fear of not finding a way out wakes me and leaves me with a sense of having seen an allegory of human life unfold: each man trying in his own way and in vain to find a way out or to brighten up his prison.

I remember another dream in a similar setting. I needed a room and someone suggested one of those hotels in which (according to the terms of the dream as I wrote them down) 'one can pass freely from one room to another'. However, after a very tall, thin, unsettling woman appeared at my table, I saw unbearable visions of sick, wounded or dying men in front of every door I passed.

ᶻ❧

Tübingen. In Hölderlin's tower, I had vaguely hoped to find the room in which he spent half of his life as he had left it, with the window where he monotonously recorded the empty seasons of his last poems—just as we do find, all the same, something of Michel de Montaigne in his library or of Jean-Jacques Rousseau in Les Charmettes. But there may have been nothing left to save by the time Germany's interest in him awoke. Whatever the case, the few engravings, the books behind glass, the room with its carefully waxed floor, the repainted walls could only frighten away his shade, if it were still tempted to prowl around here.

But quite nearby there are those coloured houses overlooking the Neckar River, in the middle of which lies a small island planted with tall plane trees. And at the foot of these houses, the largest of which is the famous Stift, there are terraced gardens—today their paths are full of mud—which the owners reach by climbing precarious wooden ladders. And there, outside, under the clouds, in what remains of the tender and untamed in these gardens between the river and the old, noble houses, on the lawns cared for by students, hovers a kind of eternal intimacy—a harmony that resonates here and there in Hölderlin's poetry.

Munich. Aside from our hosts' friendliness, I remember little more of the city than a sense of enormous void, vast spaces at regular intervals, empty and bleak: large squares, huge construction sites, broad streets. The ruined Army Museum they had wanted to leave as it was in the middle of a grass-covered square, built of dark brick and cement, was more beautiful than many neo-gothic or neo-classical buildings that had been restored. It rose like a massive phantom, filled with meaning and menace, a symbol of defeat, of disaster, of absence.

There is, then, this: those bleak voids, one after the other, those phantoms, all those revivals of the nineteenth century: colonnades, ogives, triumphal arches, monuments to victories; and, at the Hofbräuhaus, to the sound of a popular ensemble in shirtsleeves—accordion, piano and trumpet—whose gestures an ecstatic child imitates at their feet, massive men, like species of oxen or pigs, with strong heads and heavy features, enormous waitresses, red and drenched in sweat, as ready for insults as for laughter, songs that burst out and die down suddenly like bellowing, fists pounding rhythmically on the rough wooden tables into which passing Americans stupidly carve their names. The brutality of the Song of the Nibelungs transposed to a large working-class city, after many wars and violence infinitely more horrible than all the massacres in that epic.

I know that, like many others, I have not necessarily retained the best from the Alte Pinakothek, that prodigiously rich museum, but only the art stirred in me a feeling more profound than my simple taste for painting. For example, Poussin's *Apollo and Daphne*, which treats the same subject as his last, unfinished painting, but with far fewer figures. The freedom with which Poussin has painted them and the power of the shadows, reminded me of his *Inspiration of the Poet* in Hannover.

What first draws one to this painting are the accents of dark blue (under the clouds), rust-brown, yellow or gold, and the golden light in a deep sky, as well as the entire painting's tonality at once dark and warm. I think it touches one first with its imposing harmony, grave, rich and noble. To this is added the serenity of a triangle composition that celebrates exaltation, that of the standing feminine body, and melancholy, that of an old man (Peneius?), who is a river, covering his eyes and letting the glittering water flow past his feet. Finally, there is the couple that reveals at the same time closeness and distance, the grace and cruelty of love, and the mysterious intrusion of the foliage, like flames come to protect the hunter's prey.

❧

Hugo. In *Things Seen: Dandelion . . . A soap bubble of the meadows that seems to have been blown by the earth.*

Fields. Solitude.
And if, by chance, a swarm of bees passes by behind a hedge, you hear a murmur in the air like the drone of a big city.

Death: *I bend over this shadow in which I see, in depths that would be terrifying were they not sublime, the white light of the immense eternal dawn.*

November

After months of almost total silence, in near impossibility or incapacity, against a hundred difficulties that I push aside, that I try to push aside by ignoring them, blindly, therefore, gropingly, in obedience to a vague feeling, to what is left of a feeling of necessity, to a faint hope (?) or to a vague surge of pride, of dignity—also against almost all recent literature—in the thought that there is, all the same and after all, *something else*.

By turning back within myself, closing all books except for the book of things, the book of life lived, the concrete, material, painful, secret book, I first note the traces, the lines inside me, courses that carve their furrows inside me. Images that sink into the past or that float near me, round me. Inscribed on a moving floor, like the one in Rotterdam's port when it storms. Things noted down at random and almost lazily, without paying too much attention or stopping.

꙳

The *Women Regents* of Franz Hals. An old woman who has nothing left to look at but death, who trembles, who is like a bundle of dried sticks—and whom almost nothing reaches any more.

The balm of the trees, of the sky, of colour, balm that does not heal or no longer heals, no longer suffices.

The coming unknown that now seems to consist only of growing blackness.

To no longer know how it will be written, be expressed, being almost certain that it can't be expressed, because you cannot build with remains.

Christ, the Passion.

Words that are carried, carried almost exclusively by pity, astonishment, fear.

In the mirror, my ancestors' face, in my hand, my ancestors' pen. My mother's, my father's.

The voice no longer carried on the air; the black of the sky.

Someone who leaves without getting anywhere.

There is no longer any knowledge that suffices. Everyone seems to speak effortlessly and decisively; me, in my country, within myself, I've almost 'lost language in a foreign land'. There is almost no word left that has not lost its substance, that escapes the wear and tear of use, or else they have no connection, one to another. I would like to be able to write with the flow of the simplest words, but I cannot. What has happened to mankind? Struck by an invisible arrow, with no name.

Words like empty husks, hollow.

I loathe everything I've said that was still full of illusion and falsehood. (Builders on this dust. Builders of houses made of dust. Builders of dust.)

I should pull words out of my body, only in pain, or in fear, packed together like stones in the mountains.

Time starts digging into faces, making the gaze foggy, unclear, unfocused. The earth rises up along side us like water against the sides of boats.

Air no longer carries, enchants the countryside. Vineyards and orchards are like fires in the earth, but your gaze cannot reach them. The gaze has no more roots.

Celestial light no longer suffices or cannot be deciphered.

When the tawny owl calls in the night, it doesn't call anyone or anything. I hear it again now as I did lying next to that almost forgotten woman, but I will not follow it through the forests in my imagination; at the most, I could call as it does, no longer knowing how to turn away from the night. Oh, to be able to call like that!

And yet, I've not lost all desire to keep searching, moving forward.

❧

Large curtain, large veil of clouds, smoke above the foliage that seems to be on fire.

High veil, high, immobile smoke, what point is there in lifting it with a powerless hand.

My gaze is like an animal that can find no nourishment.

The tool is broken, the hand holding it is but skin and bones, the will controlling them has grown weak.

I am like someone no longer alive. The words and looks of a phantom, without heat, life or meaning.

❧

In the night
I rise and count my profits once again,
and my expenses.
I see that my body is ugly
as neglected aged bodies are.
I count my losses in these four walls,
I have become just like the others
who see nothing but night
and who are afraid.

❧

Dream. In Rome. A slow walk with a completely unknown woman. When I put my hand on her shoulder, she does not pull away. The joy of these first consents, the greatest joy. We go to a trattoria to drink white wine. Solicitude: is she chilly, etc. This simple moment in the street, amidst a crowd.

December

A man leaning on the wet handle of his rake forgotten in the rain and contemplating the fire, the hollow, the cave of fire.

❧

Tawny owls call to each other, several at the same time, almost every night. This is the bird I believed, or wanted to believe, was the barn owl of my poem, almost twenty-five years ago in Sèvres. To say that I hear it differently now would be an understatement. Despite the thoughts of death in that poem, it opened itself up entirely to the expanse of the future. Now, it is probably true that there is no longer a place for a poem of any kind because the illusion (?) of ties between the worlds has been destroyed, because there is no expectation of anything but decline. And yet . . . There is still this 'and yet' that has no more force than a glance. There is still increasing ignorance.

And the beauty of a winter morning through the cold windowpane of the heart.

❧

Clear, windless days, mild afternoons in the walls' shelter. Mornings before the day: Venus.

The pink, the violet of evening that rises like a tide in the narrow gardens.

1973

January

On the lakeshore in N., the day after Christmas, the flight of a raptor, perfectly visible in the frost-covered, diaphanous forest. As if we had surprised it in a life ordinarily hidden.

&

Down below the cemetery, a lively stream. Between yellowed, but already reawakened, grasses, this quickly flowing and in some places sparkling water, this joyful water in its bed of dark earth. The blind sky like a window.

&

I'm surprised that Roger Martin du Gard, convinced positivist that he is, does not say one word in his correspondence with Jacques Copeau, with André Gide or with his daughter, about technique, about science or about the already visible changes brought by advances in these fields. These are two worlds ignorant of each other. Was that not as important, in the end, as politics?

&

In Abbé Huc's book on his travels in China, the story about the House of Chicken Feathers, that huge dormitory for beggars of all ages, with its floor covered in chicken feathers. An equally huge blanket, with holes cut out for the sleepers' heads, was lowered onto them every night with pulleys.

The Abbé's entrance in the courtroom where the accused, suspended from the ceiling, was being whipped so violently that the judge leading the missionaries had to lift his robes as he walked through the blood.

His story about the frenzied gamblers who gamble away their clothing and are thrown outside, naked, in the most extreme cold. They try vainly to warm themselves and die of cold under the laughter of those who had more luck. And the story about those who go so far as to bet their own fingers and how they chop them off, then and there.

❧

The weather is a bit colder. Steam clouds the windows unevenly. Through them, you can see a pink line, a sky that will be clear. You can hear someone filling a bucket of coal. No divinity rises, stretches, behind those mountains any longer.

❧

Sometimes I think I can hear everywhere only phantoms' talking, the 'shadows' chirping' that Henri Thomas wrote about in *Sainte Jeunesse*.

I remember the visit of that young man, completely friendly, as a matter of fact, who was studying drama at something that can hardly be called a school and spoke to me about it. I couldn't help but find what he said dreadful—like almost all of today's new art forms. He seemed unable of more than just talk about the Sacred. I finally told him that I was moved by his no doubt fruitless hope of recovering the Sacred by borrowing simultaneously from several forms of sacredness, an inversion of the true way. Their critical spirit is not being developed, to say the least, and their bases are foggy, like the mountains on certain days. But the need that drives them, in reaction to an almost unbearable world, is moving. The combination that is sometimes made of science and these muddled impulses is hardly more serious.

❧

These late afternoons of winter have a crystalline fragility on a dark background, something for which the word 'violet' might perhaps strike the right note.

❧

Evenings of pink wood. On the slopes lining the road, the fire's teeth.

Samuel Pepys' *Diary*. First of all, the tone amuses. It is the completely neutral tone of a schoolboy carefully composing his lessons. Pepys' era was certainly less sentimental than ours. Today, we become indignant at the harshness with which Madame de Sévigné speaks about people of modest means. Pepys attended the torturing of men Charles I had condemned to execution without evincing the least horror; he simply notes that from his vantage point he could see on one side of him the heads of the two condemned men displayed in a corner of the roof and on the other side, a very lovely view. Then he goes to eat and drink as usual, large amounts, in other words. You can't help but think that men of that time had stronger constitutions than we do now. Pepys often got up very early, at four or five in the morning, which did not seem exceptional to him, and went to bed late. His menus included enough for three meals today. Bribes are par for the course: Pepys never refuses them, he simply pretends not to notice them. Nothing delights him more than watching his revenues grow. Periodically, he decides to fast, giving up the theatre, sex or drink, charging himself fines if he fails to keep them. He always finds reasons to excuse his lapses, especially with the theatre (he considers Shakespeare's plays to be generally inept).

Pepys' demeanour recalls certain characters by Molière, for whom he could have served as a model. In his *naivety*, his candid self-satisfaction and recognition of his faults, he closely resembles George Dandin, Monsieur Jourdain and Harpagon. The scene in which he feverishly digs up the gold he had planted in his garden and panics when he can't find all his coins because he hadn't taken the time to store them in caskets before burying them is worthy of *The Miser*. As is the scene in which he promptly and discreetly slips back into his pocket the silver he had brought for the baptism of his godson when he learns, with a sharp sense of pique, that the child was not named after him. His efforts to educate himself, his vanity in dress and his dreams of living in high style are pure Jourdain. And this confirms that we have here the portrait of a world that could have been found in London as easily as in Paris.

March

Gare Montparnasse. The train for Nogent-le-Rotrou is packed. Across from me is an elderly couple with pleasant faces. The husband, who is keeping his wife company until the departure, rests his hand gently on her knee. They speak with unreserved affection, while two young people kiss each other without reserve and a fair amount of noise. A little boy, dumbfounded, discreetly draws his mother's attention to them with his eyes. When the girl got off the train at Versailles, she turned on the platform towards the window with a luminous smile. It hadn't even occurred to the young man to look out.

❧

Return from Paris in a compartment with two salesmen from the north of France. An old man who 'did both wars' and is still able-bodied. He is going from Charleville to Montpellier to visit a niece he has not seen for fifteen years. He wouldn't need much encouragement to tell his entire life story. Having lost his wife a year ago, he complains of being lonely and of the difficulty in finding another. Recently he thought he had found a gem, a good cook, clever and all that, when he realized she was turning tricks. At seventy-five. He slapped her and threw her out double-quick. He's pleased that they're tearing down the old sections of Charleville.

The other traveller, a woman from Brittany whose heavy make-up only accentuated her ugliness, is from Valenciennes. She also likes living in the north because of the supermarkets. The Rhone valley, which the train is following, seems deserted to her. The old man is indignant that the embankments along the tracks have not been cleared and cleaned.

When you live more or less isolated, you forget how most people think. I'm not sure that isn't an advantage.

ᨠ

The fact that I have sometimes written about certain privileged moments (hardly something new, incidentally) earned me a visit from a young painter whose ambition is to paint such moments. I wasn't able to encourage him as much as he wished. It's true that through appearances, through the course of my texts, at the end of certain texts, I had the feeling that I had reached the elemental and sometimes even a marvellous enlightenment. But can you *start* from there? I see too many poets (or painters) eager to put *first* and *foremost* what I believed I had discovered, almost without wanting to, *at the end* and *behind* things. It's the same with those who believe they can start from the Sacred or, worse, from a mixture of all the kinds of sacredness that the most superficial fashion throws together arbitrarily, like furniture from different periods.

ፈ❧

Tying up one's bundle of images, the inventory of one's meagre possessions? A ghost story. Everything clamours that there is more, reinforcing those claims with bloody evidence that soon fade, and yet we still doubt that we must reduce it all to this.

That which can be written, but not spoken . . .

(Who wrote: *I give you these verses so that if my name / Should safely reach the harbour of distant years . . .* ? It sounds like Joachim du Bellay, or a modern echo of Du Bellay. Baudelaire? I don't know why these verses are running through my head at the moment.)

Receive these images, receive these shadows, receive
    this smoke or this nothing.
You watch with fear as your hands change,
you feel dizzy at the thought that soon you will lose
    your grace or your strength,
collect then . . .

As the checkered magpies fly from pine tree to pine
    tree under a light rain lifted on the wind,
Show your friends these traces of ghosts . . .

The frightened child carries his map of the city
    inscribed in his heart.
A rooster, bright red and mean, runs the school,
the saddlery has a strong smell, the peony is wet,
under the lamp with green pearls shining on the
    checked tablecloth
as a hand turns the book's pages,
Siegfried rides over the drawbridge into Worms
—his horse is whiter than snow—
a forgotten voice deciphers his barbaric story through
    the Gothic script,
soon he will fall, a spear in his back, near the stream,
    among flowers.

Things don't go the way we think, we do not live
    coherent, logical stories
surrounded by familiar faces . . .
People are so far away and do they even have faces?
    Did we forget them, never see them, or were their
    faces hidden?
In any case, the memory retains nothing whole.
Where were they? Where were we?

The flowers are closer sometimes, the box tree hedge,
    an old object becomes a talisman.
Certain places are closer, a wall with espaliered trees, a
    small round temple in a garden,
and when you step out from the dark streets,
the Arsenal, blind behind its grille,

the sawmills in their sheds, their golden dust floating
between the station and the cemetery,
or the prison's high wall with its small, dark barred
windows, towering over the river.

The Broye did not stop flowing in the fog,
on Sundays the rifle shots echoed off the greenish
cliffs.
A couple grew old waiting for a letter from America.
Four sisters fanned themselves in the closed-up house,
one wanders in a pink camisole on the vaulted
staircase,
the other was put in the asylum where she paints
bouquets,
the oldest, dressed in black, has red cheeks from
standing at the stove all day,
and won't Sophie drown herself because of a broken
heart?
But the father chuckles and his obese body shakes.
At teatime they take old biscuits from a cupboard
painted red inside.

What are you doing there? You're neither happy, nor
sad, surprised perhaps,
and you consume more images than bread . . .

April

The very beautiful forests of holm oaks, when the trunks are covered with pale green lichen, the old wood is brittle, rotten. Invisible wild boar. Trees like stone, shade, very old walls.

I never fully grasped the meaning of those places. I only guess that one finds in them a confusion of trees and ruins, a sense of something ancient, long-lasting and solemn, to which the trunks' almost livid shade of green adds a more elusive, essential element. Countryside for the trees of the dead, where the borders between worlds seem fainter than elsewhere.

❧

Pablo Picasso is dead. The papers put him on the same level as Michelangelo, Francisco Goya, Diego Velasquez. In doing this, they ignore a decisive difference. Picasso was perhaps a kind of genius, but a genius of a period that was hollow at the core. This produces a strange kind of genius, one who dazzles and stuns without convincing.

❧

Rilke's *Letters*. His excessive refinement of sensation can sometimes be irritating and even more so his life doctrine which was primarily a way of safeguarding his freedom. But the poet is present in almost every passage. His letter on New Year's Eve in Capri. The profundity of what he writes about Vincent Van Gogh, about Paul Cézanne, even though his eye was educated in the north, in Worpswede, where the painters were very mediocre.

❧

The poplars near Valaurie with their first hints of green. On the right, barely yellow or beige, but above all luminous—and the word is not exact; traps for sunlight (but that is even less accurate). A rejection of metaphors, not wanting to betray a more mysterious simplicity.

Illuminated poplars. Lighter poplars, sunlit. The grass darkens under the sunlit poplars here and there in the valley. And nothing is said.

❧

'To be naked is to be speechless,' says the Dogon sage in Marcel Griaule's *Conversations with Ogotemmeli*. The need for masks, the need for words. In another passage, the description of the spirit who is both a weaver and a speaker would have thrilled Francis Ponge with its precise, almost mannerist text–textile comparison: the spirit's teeth being those of a weaver's reed, the yarn the word, etc.

ॐ

The fig tree's budding leaves, like so many goblets used as lanterns or nightlights, letting the light shine through yellow.

May

Swelling greenery, growing too quickly like a sudden tide, almost sad in its swiftness, its haste, but for another reason also, something heavier, with more shadows, something closer to rain, less 'native', less 'beginning'.

Chestnuts draped in green feathers under a warm, panting wind and dust-filled sky. Dandelions, meadows seen in childhood with a mysteriously desolate eye—as if it all were empty or forever inaccessible.

Green leaves, a too-sudden flooding
already too heavy, too damp
the clouds' green sister
and the yellow flowers
invading the fields
held in the child's desolate gaze
as if the future
as if the entire world
were painted on a void.

(Colours as bitter as medicine.)

All of a sudden, filled with fear in broad daylight
facing the painted meadows
over which only rootless shadows flit.

The swelling, almost exuberant greenery can also inspire a feeling that is the opposite of impoverishment—as if to prove at the same time that none of the comfort that leaves or colours provide can banish distress or dread.

❦

She sits, curled up like paper too near a flame. One hesitates to speak of this, to speak of it is almost odious, and yet it too is a part of what is essential.

❦

What is the night? And the man who burns brightly in night's darkness?

❦

Birds call before daybreak, loud and urgent near the house, clearer and less frequent far off—marking distance like trees in a field.

❦

I am astonished by how few memories remain from each period of my life and by how vague they are. Like that hotel room on Rue d'Odessa—the weak light bulb and the mirror on the ceiling, the rattling trains—but what else? As if I had been living in a dream.

❦

Dream. A walk in a large city. Suddenly I find myself in an enormous building, very old, grey or off-white, and very empty. I point out its beauty to others. Then the scene shifts to an interior courtyard; a man on the second floor is refusing to come down. The police are trying to take him into custody. I help them by climbing the stairs. From his doorstep he throws things into the courtyard below. He is armed with a pitiful knife.

A third, stranger scene follows. In a kind of enormous, empty attic there is another man who is waiting for the woman I am with in order to do to her what he has done to the others: murder her by scalping her quickly and suffocate her by stuffing her under the floorboards, then throwing her through a trap door and locking it again. An attempt is made to capture him. His behaviour is explained by the fact that he had been buried alive during the war.

September

Le Tertre. Morning. Western view. The large field with oxen had fascinated me before, on my first visit in 1959. It sloped down from under the terrace to a stream hidden behind trees. Beyond, a forested ridge. The ivory-coloured oxen did not seem to move about randomly over the course of the day. Now, as the shadows begin to retreat from the upper end of the field adjacent to the Tertre, they climb in a diagonal, grazing on the spare, dry grass, as if they were following the sun; flocks of starlings escort them or lead the way. Then the movement stops and they gather into groups. Some of them lie down. Others stand in pairs, rub their noses against the others' spines, occasionally attempting a laborious, spectral coupling. Their slowness when they lick each other or stare straight ahead makes them seem farther than they are and caught in a dream. At the bottom of the field a few isolated trees provide some meagre shade, where they will find refuge later in the day.

On the terrace's lawn, herds of Venus' birds—when they take flight, there is the sound of clapping.

When the oxen lie down, their horns are sometimes more visible, not always, bending back at the top. A magpie walks on the forehead of one of the oxen, stays there a while, goes about its business and the ox does not move. The oxen chew their cud in the sun, lying like tombstones or the funerary monuments of Chinese emperors. Immobility reigns over the entire countryside under a sky of blue mist. Were it not for the distant motors and the wind in the great trees, the silence would be total. No lowing. These herbivores with their white pointed horns are serene.

Southwestern view. The marvellous large trees form a line above the pond as in a canvas by Poussin, that painter from Normandy. In the landscaped opening between the two groups, you can see Bellème on the top of its hill, like many market towns in the morning, carved in crystal from the light mist by the sun. How clear it all looks, how peaceful! And how distance and the morning light deceive the eye! They deceive and still, their deception exists in grey, shades of blue and pink. Everything seems suspended, light as well as enclosed. You can still see it. Someone who works behind these windows here knows he will not see this again next year and yet doesn't howl in desperation or revolt—yet he still thinks of it all and of others with kindness and consideration.

In the park, the alleys lined with various trees, each has its own particular colour, its own amount of shade. They protect one's thoughts or daydreams marvellously well.

Doves, seen up close, look ridiculous; they traipse along like coquettes with their parasols from the era of Proust. They puff themselves up and nod constantly: a subject for Jules Renard. But they are also, and primarily, something else if one considers them only in flight, the shapes of the flock, their white spots. One forgets that they are busy feeding themselves. Their wing beats snap like flags at a celebration. They have never appeared stranger, more beautiful, more expressive to me than they did this spring, in the mornings when I rose early and noticed them in the mist still floating over the lawn.

October

Death of Ingeborg Bachmann, burnt alive in her bed by a lit cigarette. She was someone who was always teetering, as if about to fall into every trap, every abyss. She was at once extraordinarily closed in within herself and open to impressions and aggressions from the outside world. It is horrible to have to say that the fire in which she died is one she could have imagined and described horrifyingly well in her books.

November

Dream. Half-way up a very large stone stairway in an old city, I meet Miss R. in a coat and blue hat of a bourgeois elegance that suited her taste when she was alive: she was very much herself. Utterly stupefied, I describe this resurrection to one of her friends from that time. Then Miss R. turned into my mother who is still alive. But in my dream she too has been resuscitated and I question her tirelessly. All I can remember is that when I asked her how she had 'lived' between then and now, she answered 'by begging'. I take her home (which is not our house, but an unknown apartment). We look for my father who is worried she won't smile at him. I've forgotten the details of this dream, but it was pervaded throughout with a sense of heartrending joy. My mother, almost always lying down, sleeps in the middle of the room.

༄

C.M.d.G.'s burial. Local people carry the bare wooden coffin under the linden trees and lower it into the grave dug in a spot chosen by our friend. The priest reads a prayer in Latin in low voice. The words sound elevated and reassuring and are mysteriously well-suited to the sky that can be glimpsed through the very tall, almost leafless trees that stand right next to the grave.

≥●

A large whip across the page . . . 'Language is the air's whip.' Destroying all poetic comfort.

≥●

How does a shadow speak, a kind of shadow or absence floating in winter's extreme clarity, almost hating its own transparency—only just able to destroy this crystal or to be astonished that it is possible, that it exists and that we are looking at it. Almost feeling rage or shame, the face, still dry, crosses the emptiness of the air, the garden, the air's invisible space. Under oblique Orion.

December

And the Lord said, 'Go forth, and stand upon the mount before the LORD.' And, behold, the LORD passed by, and a great and strong wind rent the mountains, and brake in pieces the rocks before the LORD; but the LORD was not in the wind: and after the wind an earthquake; but the LORD was not in the earthquake: And after the earthquake a fire; but the LORD was not in the fire: and after the fire a still small voice. And it was so, when Elijah heard it, that he wrapped his face in his mantle, and went out, and stood in the entering in of the cave. And, behold, there came a voice unto him . . . (I Kings 19:11–13).

And if he were not even in the still small voice?

The shadow's speech, the phantom's, the mist's.

❧

Fire at daybreak in the blue mountains.

1974

January

A raven ascends in a patient, slanted flight in front of the
pink clouds of dawn.

March

Do not let it pass unless you repeat this to yourself: the longest, mildest evenings, the snow soon faded into the grey that blurs mountain and sky; closer, the cool earth in the garden and, as if suspended above, the light green spiraea shrub, the day's dwelling. That cool, vigorous thing: the time just before spring. A space still large, an even greater light, the leaves' effervescence: bread for the eyes.

And do not forget the pink peach tree against the tilled earth; or other, smaller ones, between the dark cypress nurseries. Is there another marvel there that I've never noticed? What is it? Lightness, coolness, fragility? Should I let myself start again with the endless stomping that only destroys what cannot simply be transcribed or copied? Earth, flowers. Cypresses that can easily be called black but are not at all funereal. Like bushy ramparts against fires that are not fires. I think what catches fire here is time, its passage—the way it ignites in everything yellow. And the earth below, behind, is what is ageless, not abstractly eternal, but it is what endures, the expanse.

Meanwhile, the chestnuts are budding precociously.

The flower that pierces the hard bark of the ground, that splits rocks.

No doubt there is, indeed, something in this connection, this relationship between flowering trees and time, the swiftness of time: that which takes fire from the rapidity of its flight. But be careful not to push too hard in this sort of 'translation'. The allusion must be slight and swift. You must still sense the air, the gardens, the clouds—and the marvellous March rain, so brief, unexpected and fruitful. *Quick*: the word *quick* has a connection here too. And yet, no haste, no fervour. Difficult. Nothing is more difficult. Not the flesh, nor the angels, nor dawn—despite the temptation to resort to these comparisons. Every spring, I find myself caught in the same loop, the same trap. Just the other day, from the train before Tarascon, I saw the beauty of the large orchards surrounded by cypresses, the trees just touched with purple against the high black fences—which the great expanse of these orchards made even more striking. There was a birth (dark, silent) of colour, as when fire ignites. There was solemnity, too. Should one think of music? The enclosures of cypresses impose a form on this landscape. What troubled and confused me in the eastern Pyrenees was the absence of this rigour. Rilke wrote of this in connection with Toledo: some landscapes seem to have begun on their own, within themselves, the 'realization', the transposition the painter would have imposed upon them were he to tackle them. Their spiritual meaning already shows through, decanted, within them. They are mirrors that sometimes show us our hidden faces.

꤮

What first struck me on reading Carlos Castaneda's books, in which he relates his encounters as an anthropology student with the Indian witch doctor in Mexico who eventually initiated him into 'consciousness', is the quality of his narrative. It remains consistently sober and avoids the three stylistic dangers that threaten this kind of book: the scientific, the journalistic and the lyrical. (Understandably, Castaneda's books have since gained an extraordinarily passionate following.) I occasionally had the impression, at the time (when I read his first two books in French translation), that he went further 'poetically' than did Michaux in his 'poems' inspired by similar experiences.

His account of picking peyotl in the mountains, dated 6 July 1962, for example, reminded me of both D. H. Lawrence's *The Princess* and Paul Celan's *Conversation in the Mountains*. This is a vague, unthinking comparison, certainly, but justifiable because in both of these very different texts there is the anticipation of a decisive event connected to a mountainous landscape, to the idea of a mountain pass, of crossing a boundary. (Such situations, wherever I find them, must awaken in me, if not memories then at least very profound dreams for them to touch me, to amaze me to this extent. Yves Bonnefoy examines them in his own way in *L'Arrière-Pays*.)

I'm not entirely sure how much credence one should give accounts of these experiences. Nevertheless, some have obvious affinities not only with archaic myths but with poetic experience, and some of the pronouncements the author credits to the witch doctor could have been made by Martin Heidegger or a Zen monk. On the other hand, the narrator's joy, his confidence and, more profoundly, his way of opening up new perspectives reminded me more than once of André Dhôtel, particularly in his passage on ravens and his extraordinary experience of the tilled hillside in *Voir* and the associated lesson on how to hear the 'sounds of the world'. 'There is nothing to understand. Understanding is a very small matter, absolutely insignificant.' These words of Don Juan, the witch doctor, are they not literally, even in tone, those of Dhôtel?

ε♣

Mantua . . . At midday, under grey skies. At first you see the lakes formed by the Mincio River on both sides of the city. Several boats are floating there (as they do in the background of Andrea Mantegna's *Death of the Virgin*), black, motionless, empty—or with a fisherman sitting upright, black and just as motionless. Grey fog bathes the entire city, silent at this hour and almost deserted. Each time you enter one of those Italian squares, so little changed by time, you are touched, exalted, as if some very distant beauty were finally returned to you. Amazement soon turns to melancholy; even more so in Mantua because of the memory of Virgil, because of those indefinite lakes and the palace that is much too large and too empty, where the humidity eats away at the walls, wears down the columns, erases the frescos and freezes the visitors' steps. Virgil . . . Just then, on a high, marble plaque attached to the facade of a *palazzo*, I reread the verses from Canto VI of Dante's *Purgatorio* depicting the miraculous encounter of Virgil and Sordello:

> *But see, there, a solitary soul.*
> *Sitting alone, he is looking at us:*
> *He will show us the quickest way . . .*

Only this language is worthy of these tall, severe residences, like those in Mantegna's paintings that associate the history of the Gonzaga family with trees, horses, monuments and the sky, even finding place, beyond the family's destiny, which seems more weighty than joyful, for the dream evoked by any opening into the distance.

May

It isn't possible to write every day at set hours, the way a farmer tills his fields or a clerk pages through and annotates his accounts. Rather, you're trapped between two aversions, the one of writing the way you write (and not being able to write better or differently) and the other of not doing anything at all, which is worse. You could change professions, but that, in all likelihood, is utopian. Words, then, should clear a path between these two dissatisfactions, in the narrow gap where they find little nourishment, little heat. And yet, the air and space round us separate one thing from another so expansively and they can be so easily crossed.

October

In Canto III of *Il Paradiso*, Dante is in the moon's sphere:

> As through translucent and polished glass, or a
>   stream
> Clear and still, flowing not so deep
> As that its bed is dark, the shape returns
>
> So faint of our mirrored features,
> That, a pearl against a white forehead would
> be more visible; many such faces I saw,
>
> All longing to speak; from them I conceived
> A delusion contrary to that which lit,
> An amorous flame 'twixt the man and pool.

The way he makes tangible what is almost invisible—the souls in the heavens—is simply exceptional. Thinking he is seeing mere reflections (the features of a face in the water, less distinct than a pearl on a white brow), contrary to Narcissus who takes a reflection for something real, Dante turns round to find what is being reflected and sees nothing. But it must be said that Dante's art surpasses itself as his subject matter becomes more elevated. In all respects, there is nothing higher in all of poetry than certain verses of *Il Paradiso* in which the light and the voice merge.

(The closeness of French and Italian makes it tempting to try and retain his rhymes in translation, but this is impossible. I think one should prudently abstain.)

‡

We certainly can no longer hope to see the same light that Dante tries to fix in his sight as he rose ever higher towards the end of his book. And yet, we have seen one that is perhaps not too inferior to his—we catch sight of it unexpectedly in our space and time—just as pure, as heartrending, but it is no longer a part of a sovereign order that can encompass the Universe. It is as though this light were straying through ruins, wild like weeds.

‡

A moment of astonishment: the sight, once again, of the black, crystalline, winter sky, filled with stars, while thinking of the verses in *Il Paradiso*, of Dante's journey through the nine spheres of heaven.

1975

April

Ravenna. One must return here and stay for a long time, wandering, reading books or chronicles of past eras; because there is something here that you cannot find in other Italian cities, something that the city's rather white light and almost somnolent peacefulness preserve—or at least help you perceive even over the course of much too brief a visit. This tranquillity is not that of a city reduced only to tourism and reminds me a little of the beauty of Aigues-Mortes. It produces a sense of distance, of remove; as much in the streets round San Vitale, for example, as inside the church, and round the Mausoleum of Theodoric or the Basilica of Sant' Apollinare in Classe. It is the distance of dreams. It prevents you from seeing the churches in Ravenna as museums. It prepares you for the silence that, inside, becomes effortlessly more profound.

੨੬

Hotel Rosa, Milan. In the absolute silence of three o'clock in the morning, in a desert of cold stone, the song of a blackbird.

*

May

The swifts' shrill or whistling outburst draws your atten-
tion back to the height of the sky.

June

Here too, the absolute silence of three o'clock in the morning, the 'little hours' of night as Paul Claudel would say, except for the sound of the alarm clock like a saw, chewing up time. Night. I can light the lamps, but their light is cold at this hour. It doesn't help. I can go downstairs to another room, but I will not escape the night. There is no way out. I will stay within its walls. Only time will help me out when it paints, bit by bit, the day on the walls (and therefore, I won't really have got out)—but this image is thought rather than felt, because dawn will in fact be more like the opening of a door in these walls—even if, on reflection, day is painted on the black of night.

ào

Dream. I can only remember what seems to be the ending. We (I don't know who is with me) are invited to watch birds hunt in the clear morning air from a window or a high balcony. There are two birds, a kind of pigeon or dove, flying at different heights through the sky. The lower one, which I notice first, beats its wings then hovers motionless for a long time with great elegance. I then turn my eyes to look at the higher one, almost at our level, closer and more easily seen. The memory of the hunting birds in Góngora might have flitted through my mind at the time. The thought that we had finally seen how these birds hunt gave us a feeling of immense satisfaction, even joy. The higher bird alternately moved its right wing, then its left, slowly, almost solemnly (like a priest at mass). Soon, I noticed with surprise that it was 'standing' in the air, in a position no birds ever assume. Looking down, I saw that the lower one was a woman standing upright in the air, mimicking the same slow, infinitely peaceful and serene gestures like a benediction. This woman was not young, as I might have hoped, perhaps I regretted it on waking, but was a sort of nurse or nun already somewhat advanced in years, in a grey and white robe like a pigeon's plumage, with grey hair and a slightly wrinkled face—she wasn't old, either, nor was she someone I had seen before.

And then, or perhaps at the same time, or maybe even earlier, I don't know, I found myself playing a piano made of unfinished wood with its keys spread out in several rows like a typewriter, all of them completely irregular, more like the jacks of a harpsichord though some of them narrow, others wide, with ends that were squared off or rounded. On it, I was playing marvellous music that accompanied and mimicked the birds' flight and was at the same time a song of the most vivid amorous tenderness. The audience behind me was quivering, shuddering with joy. I couldn't stop playing even though the piece was finished. The exaltation grew. A whole chorus of triumphant voices rose behind me as I kept on playing and the dream ended.

Unschooled as I am in this field, I believe that what psychoanalysis would assert about this dream is that I represent the successful act of love, that the nun represents my mother, for example. Even if I were to accept such an interpretation of the 'origin' of those images (and why not?), I would be careful not to let this explanation erase the images themselves—the birds, the sky, the height, the morning air—and the nun (with regard to her, even in the dream I expressed my satisfaction at seeing such a miracle, the reality of which I didn't doubt for an instant; it may be that in the dream I had thought of Castaneda)—and the music. It is the same with dreams as with poems: they cannot be reduced to whatever feeds them in secret, which they hide and transfigure, intentionally or not.

August

The morning light gilds the spines of the large books.

September

Marvellous late summer days, still hot and windless, when the light has a milky sheen; a feeling of suspense, of delay, of a commuted sentence. A yellow leaf, fallen from the vine onto the marble table.

࿃

Wandering through the ruins of great poems, straying from one to the next, searching briefly for support, then, discouraged, closing the loosely hanging doors— Garcilaso de la Vega, Guittone d'Arezzo—unable to stop anywhere; literally disoriented, having lost the rising sun, the morning, the strength of beginning . . . This too I could try to express.

October

The strange difficulty of being almost incapable of *feeling* anything without immediately thinking of its poetic 'use'—this condition is irritating in the long run and could finally result in not being able to feel at all for fear of falling into this trap—an extreme example is the anecdote of Goethe tapping out rhythms on his mistress' back.

In other words, something odious, or at least exasperating, occurs in which attention focused on the world and encouraged by a certain poetic effort would, after a time, end up altering, if not destroying, your emotional capacity. You see a leaf fall from a shoot on the vine, and all of a sudden you have to see it fall on the blank page; you feel the particular coolness of morning air in autumn, the clearness of the sky, the sheen of light on the grass and the trees, and you cannot enjoy them without the poet rising up in your head like a zealous clerk of the court and writing! At that point, you no longer want to feel so that he will fall asleep. His quasi-automatic interference, his maniacal and punctilious activity seem to falsify your relation to the world, to make them less real and to interrupt them too soon. You already see yourself reduced to closing your eyes to avoid this mechanism.

How to find a solution? I came up with one not long ago: an irruption of events violent enough to disrupt this mechanism, some kind internal or external squall. But that is to condemn oneself to waiting for the unpredictable. And what if it never does occur, or occurs too rarely, as is likely? Is there a simpler, more modest way, better adapted to my situation and abilities? Or must I resign myself to a silence that will continue to weigh on me if it lasts?

Perhaps I should accept this phenomenon or, better yet, try to ignore it if I can, to cure it with contempt. And from that point on, I could move forward again, more or less blindly, giving in to the first, the weaker impulse, to the pleasure of it, without any aim—letting the flow of sensations and thoughts pass, even if it is sporadic. Without stopping too often on doubts, fears, scruples, etc.

When the day is beautiful over the motionless trees, when the last flowers of the year venture blooms of yellow, blue and mauve, when the earth scraped by the rake is brown from so much rain: Why should I prevent this from filling me with joy and peace for a moment?

༄

And the fine summer weather returns . . .

Once more, October's serenity . . .

The air surrounds. It is something that is not. It is openness, space, it is an absence of oppression and walls: the *free* air.

The open country, barely rising at the borders, its distant borders, like a cradle.

It is the air we can't see that we drink like cool water.

The entire sky is like a large glass of water, and the air is cool, refreshing, thirst-quenching. Hedges are trimmed. The blue garden brightens and you feel as if you were climbing a ladder, rung by rung. The branches, the grass will dry in large piles that will later be joyfully burnt. The crackling of the flames in the smoke, like another kind of air, aggressive, hectic, coloured, climbing. An inverted waterfall.

Might you still light a few more fires with these leaves on the slope of time . . .

> where a sound of dark
> bells rises from the depths
> of childhood . . .

(And so it is: I am surrounded by fugitive, shattered images with no connection to each other. They fade as they pass like birds and I wish I could gather them once more lest I be the one shattered by time.)

If I still have a reason to speak,
it can only be this one: to draw the best
water from my hidden wells, to keep it from stagnating,

rotting and darkening the sky round me . . .
(The evening yellows, waxes the large, dark leaves.)

ꝫ⃒

Orange or pink hours: dawn and evening in autumn.
The small yellow acacia leaves lie on the dark earth
like immobile glimmers, mute, lighted mirrors.

ꝫ⃒

Mandelstam's poem from 1921, which begins with the
line: *I was washing myself at night in the yard* (or simply
'outside'), represents in my eyes a poetic model that
could be set against almost everything being written
today (unfortunately against my own attempts as well,
so hopelessly far from what I would like them to be and
what I admire in just such a poem). It reconciles the near
and the distant through the simplest things. It is rough
without being strained, aching but sober. Besides, for
years now no other poet has inspired in me a sense of
'great' poetry, even through translations that seem of
very uneven quality.

ꝫ⃒

A moment is like a flower that has opened towards the
east, under clouds that are themselves in bloom, quickly
carried away by a cold wind.

ૢ

Autumn trees: as if covered with yellow and white butterflies.

ૢ

Entire days of yellow and blue, almost windless, a great yellow and blue flag not fluttering on its invisible pole, scarcely a gentle beating of wings in the trees. They are quickly turning yellow, losing their leaves one by one, leaves now brittle, that crumble when touched like burnt paper. A vast calm, a widening mesh, things opening up to a more pallid, whiter light: bright smoke. The last grapes on the vine take on the colour of night. Rarely have we enjoyed such extended peacefulness, whereas elsewhere, almost everywhere else, a blind, hopeless violence spreads. Furthermore, we no longer completely inhabit this country, this light, this peace.

November

The forests of Uchaux. Kermes oaks, sumacs and, above all, strawberry trees grow there in abundance and abandon. A surprise. You'd think it a magical forest, a celebration. You imagine paradise is filled with these trees. Why? Probably because of the little sunbursts, the profusion of small oranges amidst the hard, shiny leaves' nocturnal green that evokes a childish delight, or perhaps one much more profound.

ॐ

Everything that can be written in black on the page and that we therefore don't have much desire to write down. The silence that is the cold. I hardly escape from the flaws I denounce in the poetry of my contemporaries (fatigue, aridity, nihilism). Mandelstam, on the other hand, avoids them completely: *Moscow sleeps as in a wooden casket . . .*

Before day, a pale orange sky, salmon-coloured under grey clouds that blush reluctantly.

ॐ

On the flank of Mont Ventoux, a crest of white clouds rises along the ridge of a little valley.

࿔

The moon, visible in broad daylight, in a pale blue November sky over old gardens, moist earth.

࿔

Seven o'clock in the morning. The first bird cry spins like a rattle, briefly, breaks off, spins a bit longer, pauses, screeches again for a few seconds. I don't know what species has such a voice in the morning. It could almost be an insect, it's so dry and mechanical. (Perhaps a woodpecker drilling into the bark?)

Such noise no longer announces the arrival of lepers.

࿔

The noise of yellow aspen in the quarry, like a stream.

࿔

No light, do not turn on the lamp, the better to see the break of day in its true light, to enjoy its birth and its fading.

From the window, read the signs, the page of the sky. Grey strips bordered with black on the lower edges blanket the east and the colours of a bland dawn are visible only to the south, there where the sky touches the horizon in an opening shaped like a cup, a chalice. The whitish smoke of the first fires billows, the smoke of the elderly who have difficulty rising; the wet asphalt shimmers between the last leaves. You hear the noise of motors and the call of a lone rooster.

 è♣.

In the quarries of Saint-Michel: views seen through dark trees (pine and holm oak), views of small villages, Solérieux, Montségur; harmony of the fields and the tilled earth, green and brown, green and ochre, green and red—shading into purple. Another harmony than those noted in the past (green and pink, blue and yellow), the deepest (wintry), though not at all cold. On the contrary, at first you're tempted instead to say hot, deep like bass notes and nevertheless resonant, peaceful, mute, calm. Not inspiring exaltation, delight or amazement so much as reassurance. (Winter, the serious season.) Profound, deeply resonant—preceding all thought of plants and earth. Evening colours—those that come before darkness—but not like the last blaze of sun on the autumn trees—something lasting, motionless, something one can stand on, a foundation.

As if the plants here grew from embers, were suited to them. Seeds heated on these braziers, bursting, sending out little green tongues and soon covering the burning layer with their coolness. Carpet. Horizontal tapestry (with mute, solid colours). Under a sky dominated by grey in various shades of darkness.

But the word ember is still too ardent.

There is iron in this earth. This earth is rusted. And yet, this reference, although scientifically more accurate, misleads even more.

To the touch, this earth is cold. Nevertheless, I continue to believe for now that the idea of *fire* is present in the background (a feeling of it, rather), a fire that would have become earth, that would have calmed and extended itself into earth, that would have grown in the guise of earth.

The grass' tomb, the grass' cradle.

December

Work in the garden. The sun sets around five o'clock.
Daylight lasts until six. The mountains' blue turns
darker. There is pink in the woods and in the sky. It is
not clear if the white is the belly of clouds or the first
snow of the year. Pink, blue, white, brown. In winter,
there are strange combinations at this hour. It is at once
dark and luminous, deep, light, cold and tender. The
snow (or the belly of the cloud) illuminates like a bare
lamp in a pink and blue room. (There is, don't forget,
the wooden side of winter, buildings of wood, timbers
covered with the patina of time, all the associations one
has with wood: solidity, roughness that is also human,
'goodness'.) You are, perhaps, in some sense inside a
forested room. It is evening, cooler, darker, deeper than
day. This brown and this almost metallic blue make up
the foundation of things: wood and iron—and in one
spot there is a white sheen like a bare lamp, in other spots
pink gleams like remains of the sun. And the snow rather
resembles the midnight moon.

❧

Mozart's *Quintet K. 516.* It seems to rise from the depths
of the earth, to well up over the earth, like light revived,

like Lazarus, a pallor that spreads in waves or in the beats of pale wings: to be able to hear and see this still—in a tranquillity that is supernatural, yet simple. And other flights, whiter still, descend from above to meet it. Like the winged encounters of love.

1976

January

Evening: the wooded hillside recalls a rust or dun-coloured animal, a fox. Further on, a light mountain rises, hardly darker than the sky—while the familiar pink light returns to the air with its tender fire.

❧

(Next-to-last visit to Roud.) He moves only with difficulty now but forces himself to sit sideways on his reclining chair, without using the backrest. Occasionally, he has difficulty finding words. You could say he has trouble remaining in our world. On his desk, the poems of Emily Dickinson: he has used a picture of a robin redbreast as a bookmark at the page with a poem about this bird, a wonderful short poem he says he has been trying to memorize in English without success.

He describes worrying vision problems he suffered on two recent occasions. The first time, an orange halo appeared round his field of vision. Everything within this halo was fuzzy, which gave him an alarming sense of straying, of drifting towards another world. The second occurred as he left his optometrist and was caused by the eye-drops he been given. He was so dazzled, the parts of the street that were in the shade of the hedge were just as blinding as those in sunlight. I was struck by the concrete force of his descriptions and the apparent serenity with which he made them.

For the first time since I've been visiting him he did not come outside to see us off and did not cross the road to 'show the way', as he would say. He only offered to.

❧

Once more, these days are almost too bright (never too bright), the leaves' fire in the garden where the two-coloured flag—flame and smoke—flaps wildly in the air that is clear all the way to the mountains, through branches of trees casting faint shadows.

❧

The wind has died down and once again it is one of those pure mornings, just before sunrise, late in this season and, it seems to me, too far to the south. How can you describe the blue of the mountains under the cloudless, silvery sky above a motionless world, as you glimpse it at the end of a street, above the rooftops? It is a blue with little colour or something altogether other than a colour (of course, since they are mountains). Colour of night, of sleep (and soon, in the time it takes to change streets or to return home, it will turn pink, then gold, then will be absorbed into the dazzling light of the risen sun). It is neither light blue nor dark blue. The contours of the mountainsides are not visible, only the ridges.

(I think of this blue again today, rereading these lines—having seen it since then, but only occasionally since I lack the determination to get up early enough. Of course, one must search elsewhere than in pure colour; but the night is darker than that; the colour of night lingering at the lower edges of the morning sky? The connection with the word 'sleep' comes close to the truth of it; but there is also a form that corresponds better with the word 'surface' (or curtain, or fence) than 'wall'. A fragment of an old phrase or verse comes to mind: *Gods of sleep* . . . But in my groping it also seems to me that the association this shade of blue has with 'mountains' should not be lost. It is distant but perceptible, absolutely pure, and filled with an utterly calm gentleness, a peacefulness, a reassuring, almost tender limit. This might be the wall that could echo back to us the gods' conversations or their waking. We listen, barely untangled from the dream's thread. Someone should start walking barefoot through the wet grass, still almost black. Someone who would never come back to where I am.)

. . . Still, I had barely begun to take pleasure in the world again when the threat of old age struck once more, struck someone close to me, like an untimely reminder—like a dark bell in the clear January air.

ॐ

Noon light on the cut wood, on the bundles of sticks (lilac and fig branches, the lilac fleecy, the fig a pinkish grey, each joint encircled with a collar of small bumps, little dots and twigs branching out in the shape of a shield), warmth we hadn't even hoped for—this soft, but brittle light—shining like water on the smooth leaves of the crocus, the strawberry trees and the viburnum. I see the light on the wood, mingling with the branches that have shadowy sides like a faint memory of the night, and suddenly my childhood returns, early spring on the slopes that border the roads near Moudon. And it seems that the anxiety I felt in those days—but was it anxiety? Why did this thought occur to me? Was it a single moment that stuck in my memory or a projection onto the past?—is replaced with joy, with surprised delight and also with gratitude for this weightless light, this precursor that paints the trunks and branches pink. It is the light of awakening, of emerging, of ascension. It draws the trees, their trunks, their branches, in light. It is revealed by them. They are the instruments upon which light plays, the instruments it needs in order to play.

❧

The links between my recent works (1967–75) suddenly strike me: each one gave rise to the next like a sequence of studies, more or less approximate, but coherent (perhaps repetitive as well). They have a suite-like character, as if I had become incapable of writing an autonomous poem, one that was self-sufficient, needing no reworking, no additions. I would prefer, nonetheless, to be able to write such a poem; to return to simplicity, a greater humility, a kind of insouciance about what I write. Especially when I am once again bathed in winter's pink and blue clarity, here bright, there clouded.

੭੬

I am trying to read *Eugene Onegin* with my rudimentary Russian. I immediately think of Mozart: melancholy and joy, alacrity, weightlessness, elegance. The elements of daily life, the quick momentum, the humour, the impertinence, the dream. The same transparency, so difficult to interpret in music is impossible to translate into poetry. I finally begin to understand, if still only vaguely, why Pushkin is so admired in his own country.

੭੬

With each day, evenings grow even lighter, if that is possible, more yellow, as if help or a word were coming from afar.

As if evening were awaiting, anticipating being a face suffused with the strange inflammation of pleasure.

Ah, it lengthens, it increases, it must be even more extensive, more limpid to receive more completely the distance, the embrace of the unknown.

It lasts longer in order to be better seen, better exposed to the invisible gaze, better possessed by the very gentle lightning . . .

❧

In the morning, a dusting of snow, very fine, in full sunlight, like restless mica, like gnats of mica. They do not land but vanish before you (as if afraid?).

Later, around noon, the sun grows pale, the sky clouds over, the snowflakes are less rare, a little bigger and less glittery, but they whirl, rising as much as they fall, as is often the case here because of the strong wind. Just a few traces stick to the roofs, to the base of the walls. Shining dust, pure and cold.

❧

The beautiful orchards of Vaucluse, encircled by cypresses or poplars, near Cavaillon, Avignon, in grey, pink and straw yellow, bathed in winter light, the brittle light of straw.

(On rereading these lines, I am rather foolishly surprised by my instinctive reaction to certain places. I cannot cover those few kilometres along the highway without being amazed: a painter's response. I have written about this too often not to be tempted to abstain this time. Still, it remains unsaid, which I almost repent but certainly do regret. If one must not pass up a single chance of pleasure or reassurance . . .

It was always especially beautiful when the trees were in bloom, pink or white according to the species of trees in the enclosure. Like a spring bubbling over a stone well? It is not only cypresses that enclose the orchard. Sometimes, unless I'm mistaken, there are poplars. I would be tempted to compare these trees to musical instruments if it weren't, as always, a risky transposition. What is certain is the extreme coolness of this (buzzing) flowering and the fact that it is protected, surrounded by living trees, themselves sensitive and trembling in the wind, makes it even more affecting.

However, once the flowering was over, the orchard was still wonderful—just more rugged—because of the harmony between the wood and the young green leaves, especially the pear trees' gleaming grey-pink wood covered with a light sheen. Chains of wood, braids of wood covered with light green leaves in the shadow of the high, straight, trembling fence, all of it inhabited with air, animated by the wind.

Sometimes there would also be a hedgerow or a half-wild clump of shrubbery.

How can I translate my happiness at this sight? I'm not even close to an answer. And a bit further off and higher, behind it all, the Lubéron—an almost Greek mountain. By which I mean the plinth of a crystalline sky, an arid, rocky, thorny plinth of splendour.)

February

Baudelaire's poems: density and profound perfection. The word 'profound' is one of the keys to his work. His music truly does 'hollow out the sky'. A mixture of fiery warmth and night, indissoluble joy and sadness. There, indeed, the infinite pervades things and enlarges them, imbues them with an extended resonance. The room, the space that resembles a room: intimate, open. Poetry has a perfumed body, but also eyes. Windows, terraces, *balcony*.

≀▲

In the morning and evening, there are already signs of early spring as fragile as straw or glass, the greenery ventures into the still frigid air.

≀▲

The difficulty does not lie in writing but in living in such a way that naturally engenders writing. This is almost impossible these days but I cannot imagine another way. Poetry as a blossoming, a flowering, or nothing. All the world's art would not be able to disguise this emptiness.

Furthermore: a work's blossoming, its external radiance, if these were to weigh upon those close to you, if they were to cause unhappiness in any way, what a deformation this would be of what you thought you had desired.

છે.

The mornings, still cool, which begin these utterly peaceful, mild, luminous late February days, days usually unsettled and often gloomy. This morning seems almost entirely stained with pink, touched by a pink glow, as if mirroring an invisible rose, as if illuminated by a distant burning rose. The brightly lit walls can be seen most clearly along with the invading dark ivy that covers some of them.

છે.

The stream in early spring (a false spring) hidden under reeds like dry straw, which we discover only by its sound in the suddenly warm air. In a few days, the flowers and flies, the first butterflies will appear and the bird songs will sound from various points in the sky; and the cool, acidic grass.

March

Night (the 'other night') is often hard to get through, even on a short path, as if our inner light, weakening, exposed to too many violent and contrary gusts, was in ever-greater need of the light of day, the light outside—more magical than ever in these early spring days.

The night that brings you back, nevertheless, to a centre (painful) that contains its portion of truth, which one is often tempted to believe is the only truth. In the night, the first cries and chirping of birds before day (I think I heard them as early as five o'clock), as if they were digging holes in the darkness, as if they were cutting it, tearing it bit by bit like a cloth. A prisoner's tools, small, clandestine tools, files, scissors—and a few stones drop from the black wall, a bit of its soot. Every morning they begin again, just a few of them at first, timidly, then more and more join in, relentless, until they triumph. It also evokes a riot, a mutiny.

But their first cries are also like drops of water, trickling intermittently—the herald of melting snow, that is to say, the first signs of warmth, of rebirth, of a fortunate cracking of the ice. (These words remind me of those Russian novels in which the breaking up of ice on rivers plays an important role, one associated with Easter eve.

I should look up those passages that have stayed so vaguely in my memory: one is in an Anton Chekhov novella entitled *Easter Eve*, the other is, I believe, in Leo Tolstoy, but which novel? In any case, there must be a wonderful connection between this noise, the sound of water finally being freed, and the candles lit for Holy Saturday, the kiss at dawn, and the greeting, 'Christ is risen!'—*Ad matutinum, at the Christus venit . . .* , as we read in Arthur Rimbaud's *Season in Hell*. The feeling of daybreak is naturally linked to the absurd hope of the Resurrection.)

Finally, the birds' morning song also recalls, though perhaps less precisely, lights being lit, sparse at first, then ever-more numerous, or the first sparks of a fire about to take. Still, in this case, the colour red misleads, since everything that happens before dawn is without colour, can only be black or white or grey. It recalls the gleam of the tools, the blades, shining with water, the fog passing or, sometimes, enveloping the entire country-side, floating round the house and only dissipating under the force of the sun.

❧

The first leaves come almost too soon, when I still wished for snow, to see it, feel its movement, its slow flight, its silent, pure and maternal soothing. Now, columns of smoke.

And this pink light, morning or evening, as if the air were a petal veined with pink, as if seen through closed eyes, a pink veil.

೫

In the light of late winter, which is made of pink dust— and in the silence that seems strange, the silence of an afternoon full of vague presentiment. A flock of titmice, their colours: pale yellow, grey, light blue and black. Their northern colours, busy messengers from the north. Birds from Norway.

೫

You are more often tempted to dissemble, to divert, to sleep. It is Hölderlin's occasional wish, his sigh; it is Baudelaire's bitter desire at the end of his life: '. . . *to sleep, and still to sleep, that, today, is my only wish. A base and revolting wish, but sincere.*' You must guard against this, even if only out of a taste for logical rigour. Because it's one or the other. The choice, rigorously considered, is: either be done with it immediately and without whining, or fight immediately and without stopping and with the purest weapons still available.

೫

Rereading various poems, no doubt too quickly. How unnecessary they seem today, how limited their ability to open, even a crack, the door to the other world that is perhaps present in this one. How little they shake our foundations. Baudelaire, more than any other poet, digs deep within us. Flashes illuminate Scève's overly elaborate verse here and there, set fire to a few of Louise Labé's sonnets. Her lyre ignites like hair in the sun.

ટ

My desire to remain rigorously truthful runs up against many obstacles. A refusal or a reluctance to add to the despair that overcomes the spirit is not the least of these. However, it could be that what I call my truth is simply an error, a lack of depth or passion.

ટ

I return to the idea of 'two nights', one transparent, magical and vast, the other a prison you cannot escape. If you feel distressed lying in bed in a dark room, you get up, open the door, go down the stairs—the silence at this hour is complete—but still, the entire house remains a prison. And if you leave the house, there are still even higher walls, the immense vault without the slightest gap. Perhaps, if you were truly able to escape the confines, you would remember that the night is open; but in reality, you haven't left your bed, and the night feels like a wall beyond the physical walls, a larger and even more impassable enclosure. It becomes, almost inevitably, an image of death. Or, rather, we replace it with the more inflexible image of death, of death without dawn. For now, you can wait a while longer and reproach yourself. The silence certainly weighs on you more than it soothes you. It is like an immense, persistent void. It's almost surprising to find that it is not filled with sighs and screams of horror. There is a sense of slippage, of drift. However, as long as you are patient, you know that the wall will crumble. The birds will arrive. They are like workers who get up early and break open gaps in the wall, their zeal increasing with their progress. Sometimes you hear them like a prisoner hearing the keys that will release him, a clinking in the narrow passage.

The fatal night, the imagined night, on the other hand, is the final night, from which the birds are forever absent. (Their voices busily try to light a fire in the east—and all of a sudden it ignites. Zealous, obliging, enthusiastic little shepherds.)

The night we waited for them in vain. We couldn't find any way out. From birth we have our backs up against this wall. But these are just images: beautiful or not, always much too beautiful.

The one serious thing is premature death, death before death, death in life. We are snatched away. There is a pruning hook that slices the eyes' stem—while the nights and days continue to alternate without being altered in the slightest.

The eyes are strange things: they drink in the world and assist in its metamorphosis into images without substance, or with less substance. Sliced or used up or extinguished. How difficult everything is for each of us!

April

The cry that might be heard in the green abundance of foliage, radically different from nature's voices—literally rending, shattering the apparent order of the world, its beautiful clear light. Distress. An abasement for which there is no equivalent in the animal world. *Tigers Are Better-Looking*: if only the world brought Jean Rhys' title to mind less often.

એ•

The surprise of snow on the lilacs, lifted and chased by the wind in large flakes that melt the moment they touch the ground: wandering, voyaging. On the thousand new leaves in the orchards, the gardens and the forests.

June

Around six o'clock in the evening, the leaves turn black, the oleander flowers are extinguished, the sky turns to silver, like a mirror.

The water is a serpent liquid and swift.

July

Organ (Bach's Fantasia in A minor): those cheerful
descents of notes. They recall a mountain of ice, water-
falls or avalanches of silver—and inversely, the moun-
tain as an organ. A sudden and stark correspondence
with silver—whereas the trumpet was victorious gold.

September

Dream. I enter a boutique in a sunny old town to show to a young woman, a publisher and bookseller, a manuscript I have brought with me and which is dedicated to her (her name is on the title page). I am as timid as a beginner. Because she doesn't know me, I have to list the titles of my books, which is always embarrassing. She doesn't say yes or no and leaves me alone in the room. Across the room, an open door leads to the building's sunlit hallway. An older woman, a tenant, comes to close it. I am brushing my hand across the table to wipe off some crumbs or scattered grains of rice. I feel another wave of embarrassment at the thought that this woman, catching me at a household task, will draw conclusions about my relationship to the bookseller that may annoy the latter.

I imagine that someone who woke up after such a dream and remembered the name on the title page (which I did not) would feel a need to find this person in reality. In all probability, no such person would be found. Or it would be a woman without any appeal at all, elderly or sick . . . A disappointment of this order awaited me in the dream because, at the end, the unknown woman, to whom I'd been attracted at first, and who had spoken with young friends—I don't remember what they spoke about, but it was a cheerful, charming image—had turned into a librarian, a 'bookworm' even, in the guise of a pale and sickly old man with a moustache.

❧

Marvellous poem by Mandelstam about the 'stony Taurids'.

I flee from work, as you would turn away from too severe a mirror.

❧

Other poems by Mandelstam, taken from Aubier's anthology and translated as a morning exercise. The unexpectedness of the images: they astonish, they awaken, but their power lasts. They have no relation to the surrealists' imagery. There is a strong presence of the real. The precise references, for example, to human anatomy, the skeleton in *Century*. The streetlights, the asphalt, the telephones of Leningrad.

❧

Chinese Poems. The *Nineteen Old Poems*, very renowned in China. The poems probably date from the Han dynasty (between three centuries before and three centuries after Christ).

Remote in the skies, the Draught Ox Star
So bright shines the Weaver Girl in the Milky Way.
She raises her pale, delicate hand,
her shuttle goes clicking and clacking through
    the loom.
She weaves all day without rest,
Her tears flow like rain,
The Milky Way is clear and shallow,
The distance between them is small,
Only the width of a stream,
And yet, they cannot speak.

The poem's source is the legend of two stars, the Draught Ox and the Weaver Girl, separated by the Milky Way. The discreet linking of the constellations and the concrete work of weaving, in other words, their separation.

Another poem needs no gloss:

The departed are more distant every day,
And every day the living draw closer
As you pass the city gate, look straight before you:
You will see only mounds and hills,
The ancient tombs have been ploughed under,
Their pines and cypresses taken for firewood.
The white poplars rustle in a sorrowful wind,
Desolate murmurs weighed down with sorrow.
I long to return to my village, my home,
I dream of returning, but there is no way back.

The Way of a Pilgrim, the 'heart's prayer' that carries him through cold and humiliation in a kind of ecstasy. The forests, the *izbas*, the beggars and, suddenly, the entrancing image of a large bourgeois house in which strangers welcome him with pastries in silver baskets and in which the seats are 'very soft'.

❧

Music. The first image that comes to me is a barrier made of straw, of notes, erected against the void, the enemy. Then it's clear that this image is very inadequate.

The coolness of evening, a marvellous sensation when you open the door to the garden, but why so marvellous? In the morning as well, with the smell of mushrooms.

The archaeological site at Fayn, near Roussas. On a mound rising gently above the plain, the modest foundations of a Roman villa and the ruins of a mediaeval farm built with some of the Roman tiles. The scent of thyme is stronger, more durable than stone. An almond tree grows between the walls—and all of a sudden the masonry, the brickwork reminds me of Rome. There is also an old mulberry tree, its leaves already almost yellow. The light and the shade are equally intense.

❧

Ancient human traces carved into the rock. These signs evidence an enormous patience, a force like water's and are very moving. Basins, silos, now filled with piles of small animal bones.

Lower down, at the foot of the hill, among the vines, thousands of black shards of funerary urns.

Muggy weather and the first yellow leaves against a sky as grey as pewter.

≀▲

Old age. Is there any way ageing can be seen as a gain?

Can you honestly believe this, claim this, when you ascertain that the spirit also grows weak, gets tired, your vision weakens, etc.? (I remember, one of Góngora's late sonnets was on this topic.)

Isn't imagining that we escape age in refining the soul, etc., simply a last-ditch effort to avoid despair?

If we are only body, where can we find any consolation or compensation for old age? How will we stand, what will support us, which cane?

What keeps us upright, what invisible spine?

Or am I wrong to ask such questions?

The unsteady handwriting of the elderly, a fissure.

≀▲

Great grey sky, in some places or at some moments almost black. The closed room—and outside, all round

307

it, this other room, these walls, this high vault through which distant rains pass. Flies—and near silence. Fitful barking, passing motors, closing doors. Trees ignite in the rain.

୨ଈ

The steady sound of rain. It falls in the stiff slant of a harrow, the sun close behind. Water and sky.

୨ଈ

The vegetable gardens in the area called 'Great Meadows' have always moved me, although I don't know exactly why. They probably won't last much longer and will have to make way for those stupid houses with lawns. But for now, the path is still lined with those lovely little tool sheds with triangular pediments, each in a corner of its lot.

Aren't these gardens a little like natural rooms, with walls made of trees and furniture of vegetables and flowers? The image is overdone, but there is something to it. The pleasure children find in drawing up the plans for a house and building it with old boards. The earth here, so wild elsewhere, is put in order, is parcelled out, without being made to seem unnatural. It is not arranged, tidied up, used as an ornament. Flowers grow in rough bouquets. Some vegetables rot, others wilt. Tools are trustingly left lying about. People talk across the gardens in the evenings, after work. Or they come early in the morning in the damp autumn fog or under the first shimmering summer sun.

These are shelters, colour-filled chambers in the green enclosure. Not the colours of the orchard, but warmer or 'older' shades (gold, rust, violet), colours of gentle fire and sunset—colours you also see on willows in winter. A treasure in a chest or in a basket. There is a harmony with the world here that has been brutally disrupted elsewhere.

Something old, yes, but in a positive sense, as with old walls, or wood under the patina of time. Why? Colours that are muted but rich—the earth's old age?

Voices rise towards the distant clouds with the scents and steam of the ground, the clinking of muddy tools. You'd think those who cultivate these gardens would be better able to resist absurd modern gadgets than others (but they aren't). The spreading houses, however legitimate the intentions guiding their construction, are the symptom of a strange degradation. The breaking of a bond. When the bond was intact, there was also misfortune, to be sure, but it seemed, if one can put it so, more 'real'. Today, even misfortune is losing meaning and it grimaces.

❧

Dull, grey weather, but mild

The south wind blows. You can hear it. Things sound hollow or muffled. Joy is difficult to find, to preserve, to recover.

ঽৡ

Music: foliage of notes as shelter, a resonant wall, a porous screen, a filter. The melody, like a chain of mountains or hills, sometimes swelling gently, sometimes rugged, heroic, strained. But above all, like a line that demarcates and divides the invisible, the unknown and the dream from a child's gaze: what lies beyond it? The mirage, its power.

Also, water flowing over stones. And outside, in these damp and rather dark days, I see the rocks covered with moss and ivy as if with dark and slowly flowing water, with nocturnal water.

ঽৡ

An era of universal dismantling and summary reconstruction. You see excessive complication set in opposition to or even being combined with excessive simplification. The results are disastrous: in the level of cultural coverage in the 'media' on the one hand, in the language of professors and scholars on the other. There too an equilibrium has been upset.

October

The raven-black of mussel shells.

❧

Cleansing the sky, stars sharpened on the night's whetstone.

November

The gorge of Moulon. High flows of limpid, churning water over the smooth, yellow rocks, hollowed out into basins here and there. Rapid.

 è♠

Death of Roud. His burial in the cemetery of Carrouge (the two enormous trees at the entrance, their foliage against the cold sky).

December

Trains of low clouds rising towards the north, pale grey on dark grey, dotted with ravens—above the beautiful dark green and brown of the rain-soaked land.

ᶚ🌢

The mountains, their folds smoke with heavy clouds in white whorls. The snow has fallen low on the mountainsides.

ᶚ🌢

Dream. We had returned to Venice, A. M. and I. First, I see us again in a vast, high-ceilinged room near the sea, through which many people pass, a sort of hallway with a painted vaulted ceiling. In the dream I remember having dreamt of Venice in exactly this way, with boats visible in the light outside through large openings (like the porticos in paintings by Claude Lorrain). I seem to find this both marvellous and rather different from the real Venice. But soon my attention is drawn back to the paintings on the hall's high ceilings. I am well aware that these are the famous Tintorettos, about which I notice two things: the excessive brightness of the restoration in one of them and, overall, the abundance of lances and swords that determine the composition (as in Uccello more than in the real Tintoretto).

Then we walk along a canal. And it's there, perhaps, that we see the first big black bird perched on a post standing in the water. It looks like one of those cormorants which had formerly struck me as funereal birds because of their colour, their name (cormorant sounds like *corps mourant* or *dying body*), and because of my sick mother. The dream immediately turned into a nightmare. We found ourselves in a church, also vast and especially high, but closed in. The floor had collapsed or had been excavated and the enormous pillars, some of which were painted in a primitive style and mostly in yellow tones, rose from these hollows or holes. One of those black birds began to fly threateningly round inside the church, ready to dive at us. Later, we couldn't go anywhere without running into one of these birds. On a pier on which mothers were passing by with their children, we thought we saw one of these birds all of a sudden, surrounded by others, harmless but rather large, some kind of turkey or peafowl. The mothers began to panic. We had to board the first boat we could find to escape from this city. (I seem to remember that in the dream I called these birds harpies, or believed that is what they were.)

The end of this nightmare, or a scene from another dream that night, unfolds on a sunlit hillside, on which a field of tall, corn-like plants sits below a forest. The beautiful summer light makes it feel like we're in the mountains. A reaper is harvesting this field, with a scythe if I saw it correctly. At that moment, I take flight like a glider and turn into a bird. I fly, I triumph over the harpies—and I know (or someone tells me) that this miracle is possible because the plants in the green field were cut down.

1977

March

A dream returns me to the old house in Moudon (which we left forty-four years ago): very tall windows, a chimney and a sudden snowfall. Thin sheets of ice melt on the wooden mantlepiece and I have the feeling of saying or of hearing someone say, 'Here comes the snow . . .'

April

Six o'clock in the morning: the mountains are a perfectly smooth, uniform blue, without a single wrinkle or shadow, and yet they are not a plain surface. A sickle moon just above the mountains breaks the heart (who is she?) and the sudden hoot of an owl sounds behind the other birds' trills, a scope owl that seems to be repeating slowly, distractedly, stubbornly, the word *buée* (fog). The fig tree's first leaves open like the palms of hands facing a sky covered with a thin layer of silver.

May

A walk in Carrouge, 'in Roud's footsteps': I'm surprised by the beauty of this countryside, still slightly cold with its flowering trees. Above the forest of Combes is the site of the 'illumination' Roud evokes in the *Journal* I am only discovering now. A sparrowhawk and some ravens take up again the hunt for the *Soledades*.

❧

Yesterday, in the hot weather, a long walk above and past La Grande Tuilière: there are areas there that have remained completely wild and as if remote from everything, strangely mysterious places—with the sound of unseen water, hidden under bushes. Why this sense of mystery? As absurd as it seems, you'd think something had happened here, is happening or will happen under the young oak trees and especially in the completely peaceful clearings, filled with an unusually bright and distant light. You'd think you had entered a new world without having left this one.

❧

Braids of water in the ruts of the path, quick, transparent braids, over the pebbles, the dirt, draining from earth that was soaked with rain throughout the winter.

❧

Rains upon rains. Violent thunderstorms: the sky cracks, the sound of rocks—as if the clouds were crumbling like stones.

❧

On the edge of the Lez in flood after last night's violent storm. The cold water glitters in the truffle fields and drowns the thyme. It streams over normally dusty paths. The birds call, their songs sound more than ever like resounding water, not the sound of rain but the sound of bubbles or small waterfalls; here and there, some of them cross the expanse. They echo and measure the distant and its distances on a supernatural scale.

The water of the swollen river flows impetuously and with surprising speed. It is muddy and shakes the lower branches of the riverside trees. It makes a deafening, almost heart-stopping noise, when glimpsed from above through the thick blackish or greyish green foliage.

The dog rose seems tangled in the trees. Why do these white or barely pink flowers look so beautiful? Elsewhere, they are lifted into the air on thin stems that fall in an arc—a bride's crown with sparse leaves—

something slight and poor, tousled, indocile like a wild child (but that would anthropomorphize it too much). Utterly simple flowers, as light and fragile as the rock-rose, but more delicate, more pure—'angelic'? Child-like, rather.

The chestnut's discreet little pink chandeliers.

June

The impressive confidence Bonnefoy affirms despite
everything in his essay, *Baudelaire and Rubens*, Mandel-
stam's poems (his enigmatic *The Slate Ode*, with its
world of mountain streams, flint, air and shepherds, its
gravel paths). Giacomo Carissimi's *Jephthe*, heard again
after many years: its melody high in the air like a flock
of birds or the movement of luminous spheres, luminous
water, so high, so *searching* but it's hard to say for what,
and the inflection on *Plorate . . . montes* (*lament, oh moun-
tains*), the connection between tears and mountains, vir-
ginity and death—this stream so high in the air . . .

❧

A morning walk to the edge of the Berre on paths I had
hesitated to take as they had become so overgrown since
my last visit. Broom plants, nightingales, the last, no
doubt. Lizard orchids on the rocky slopes. You have the
sense of breaking and entering into the birds' world,
undisturbed by anyone at this hour, or just barely, by the
first peasant in his field. Clear sky, brilliant world, bluish
mountains, like shadows. The stream is loud behind the
trees, so swollen you couldn't ford it. Foam born from
the grass obstructions. An easy haste, a rapid yet sus-
tained movement, coolness irrigating the greenery.

321

August

A gathering of frantic, gossipy swallows. The wings
tremble as if they were trying to affirm their vigour, like
athletes running before a race. They are chimney swal-
lows with red throats. Comte de Buffon wrote of their
flight: 'It seems to draw a mobile, elusive maze in the
sky . . .'

&

Music that would 'reassemble the bones', rebuild them,
fuse them together again when broken. (Listening to two
violins playing Haydn outside at night under shooting
stars and thinking of old aunt H., worn down, decrepit,
whose body no longer had the strength to repair itself.)

&

Pink morning glories: risen from autumn into the bare
rosebush, spotted with white by the rains.

September

Spider webs in the morning, made visible with dew and the fog by the thousands along the embankment and the side of the road, like so many gleaming radars.

❧

On a recent evening, passing near Venterol in the car we saw hills, a waxing moon, orchards. Another place that has 'grounds for praise', in the words of Saint-John Perse, whose praise tended to be facile and redundant. There was a harmony there that struck a chord deep within me. Cradle, hearth; forge, even. A place with dark, soot-covered walls in which fruits are slowly forged, under the dim rusty glow of the lunar light. Orchards at the base of the mountains, in the blue of the evening—protected by these walls from what is distant, from the unknown—and in the sky there is that glow like candlelight.

❧

At night, confused thoughts about what I too often seem to lack or what I find lacking in contemporary French poets: on the one hand, not just the existence but the

323

possibility of a cry of utter distress or even just simple dismay such as you can still hear in Baudelaire, in Leopardi, in Hölderlin; on the other, those singular 'inflections' like those in music, especially in certain melodies of Monteverdi or Mozart, passages that till the earth of the heart, that seem to open the hinges of spaces—and make one's entire being quiver. Poetry can have this effect, sometimes in Rimbaud, for example: 'Autumn, already . . .'

November

The silent, modest life of the hamlets, in the evening, with just one light in a window—and above it the gilding, the silks, the wealth of the sky.

❧

One weak, isolated bird call, as if lost, invisible in the calm, golden light of afternoon above the ageing gardens and the dark greenery lit with sparks of flowers. (One thinks of a prick, a seam.)

1978

January

Night thoughts, mingled with dreams: a face lit up with a first love, like the shade of pink cast upon the walls on winter evenings. That which is inevitably lost and leaves both lovers with inconsolable regret.

৵

And this pink that is particular to early evenings in winter—in clouds lit up by flames or angels in the east—associated, deep inside me, with the faces of unknown women in dreams, suddenly so strangely tender.

৵

Water flows under hawthorn and bramble bushes, under reeds, the sound of a thin stream, usually invisible, during the grey day. If you were blind, you would follow its voice, its arrow, its flight. It is as if birds were hiding under the bushes too in these surprisingly lost places, just two steps from the road, with their tall grasses the colour of wet straw, bent almost double. Slightly further on, the path opens onto an enormous, forgotten meadow on the bank of the Lez.

ᨠ

Dream. An old woman is sitting with my wife and daughter under some trees by the side of the road to T. as it leaves Grignan. I look closely at her wrinkled face, shaped like a slightly elongated square, with the calm and almost hard expression of someone who is used to suffering and resigned to it. At first, I think it's Madame P. and I am about to ask if she doesn't find it difficult, living alone up there on her very large farm, since her husband died, when I realize the absurdity of my mistake. It's her husband who is a widower since she drowned in the flooding of the Berre. In reality, it's another peasant who has been ill for a long time and whose ailing appearance had recently made an impression on me. However, for one reason or another, we must return home, so I leave with my daughter. It's morning (the sun was shining on the trees and on the old woman's face). We follow the real path. There are people here and there, along with traces of a camp that is being packed up: cots, sleeping bags. Some young people must have spent the night there, in the streets, on the square. Almost immediately after this, on the ramp that leads to our house, I notice that the sky is overcast and very dark, even though my watch says it is only ten-fifteen. How can it still be so dark at this hour? And why are stars visible in the gaps between the clouds? I'm immediately gripped by an intense fear of a cataclysm: it's for real this time, the disturbance that heralds the end.

On waking, I'm struck by the peculiar sadness that colours some dreams. It's not the fear in nightmares, reasonable on the whole, but an inexplicable dark quality that weighs on some dreams even when nothing particularly sad or horrible happens (at least not obviously so), a darkness that is compact, like stone, absolutely flawless. I've never actually experienced it in real life. Perhaps encountering this darkness is what drives a man to suicide? A black ink that would insinuate itself everywhere.

February

Snow. Light from the snow shines into the room. I
remember 1942, the large title page of Roud's *Moissonneur*
(Reaper), the prose piece entitled *Dragon*, and especially
the single phrase, which for me was truly a key to
another world: 'Rose opens the window onto a pale spot
of forgotten snow, extends her arm, shivers . . .'

March

The poems—like little lanterns in which the reflection of another light still burns.

Maybe we see the pink of evening on the walls only in the coldest part of winter?

❧

The chopped wood, the fires, the cinders, the bit of grey ash produced by an oak's ample crown, an entire foliage. Ash and snow.

June

In that region of Auvergne, the grass grows thickly
against a black or violet background; that must be what
gives the countryside so much power and beauty. The
Byzantine elements in churches.

August

The Pleiades. As I was looking for this little constellation in the sky the other night, I couldn't recall if it was visible in summer and to the naked eye, and several things vaguely occurred to me. First was a phrase by Ungaretti in *Un Grido e paesaggi* (A Shout and Landscapes), taken from a commentary on a short poem, which at first sight seemed completely unrelated: *Mi soffermai poi a guardare Pleiadi, la recente raccolta di frammenti di lirica greca* (And then I paused to linger over the Pleiades, the recent collection of Greek poetic fragments). Second was a more distant memory of this word connected to the Hyades and rain, perhaps in Chappaz's translation of Virgil's *Georgics* or in Chappaz's prose. Last was the more central memory of my wonder upon seeing this constellation for the first time, like a small bunch of grapes or an earring (which sent me, immediately and inevitably, to the passage I still knew by heart of Claudel's *Cantata for Three Voices*: 'Suddenly on her bare neck, on her ear, the flash of a diamond . . .' The association of the jewel with a woman's skin, neck and hair surely was a part of my pleasure in seeing the constellation but without forgetting, on the other hand, my astonishment before the immense distance, the abyss of the night sky.)

As if to deepen this emotion, I happened soon after on what Henry Miller wrote about that same constellation in *The Colossus of Maroussi*.

❧

T. Full moon in the pink sky between the tall hollyhocks. The black mass of the rustling mountain. Young poplars. The ridgeline—cowbells, stones, silence. Marvellous night.

September

Series of nightmares. Then I awake around five o'clock and am stunned by the winter night, Orion with its nebula like a stain of fog, Sirius almost blinding. The sudden feeling: What is the point, what good are these jewels to me, etc?

እ

A walk all the way to Salles through the narrow Berre valley in the heat. A motionless world, extraordinarily silent except for the buzzing of a few insects, flies, bees. My cold shadow warms up in this radiant end of summer. Brick-red butterflies with tiny black spots on the lavender; others, the colour of lavender when they fly, their underwings spotted with an extremely subtle grey pattern—like strange, preoccupied emanations. Then gentle gusts of the south wind begin to disturb the pine branches, so lightly you don't even hear them— another emanation, but this one invisible and one that connects.

እ

Mozart's Piano Concerto, K. 488. The adagio seems to belong to the order of the stars, comparable only to these

autumn days and nights, still, silent, poured out—as if
raised to the highest altitude.

Or water that would make the cliffs open.

October

Real things, true things, yes, but far off and almost beyond reach, strange—perhaps unmerited? Things now less mixed with the quotidian than before, things that have become exceptional, almost mirages—and yet the only ones that restore the desire to write, that inspire you to take up your pen. Already almost lost, in the past rather than the future—and that is paralysing. In the time it takes to try and express them, they have already vanished, become silent. You no longer hear them. How, then, can you translate them?

❧

I would have like to have said one more thing
out of gratitude or simply out of friendship
(a voice reached me and I listened,
I was going to answer; it fell silent)
I should insist

or else speak for me, hollyhocks, if I truly am unable,
if I no longer know, if I betray what I see

tell what the wind was like that night
and the poplars (even the poplar lying in the stream),
tell how you filled the air with your colour

336

speak, you who seemed almost to be carrying
the moon in its pink dust,
the forest murmuring on the mountainside
(the forest like a bear)
and only slightly farther off, higher up
that peaceful ridge, that pure roof, that motionless
    black slate darker than the silvery sky

say it with your petals, your scent, you thin, delicate
    columns,
because before you I am at a loss for words
no longer worthy to enter this place
or stay here, abide here
as I am so far from you already
in the realm of blind moles.

November

Beautiful, immobile autumn days of yellow and blue, in a cradle of luminous haze.

ۮ

Gratitude to the sun, scattered and fading among the
    leaves of the trees,
to the morning fog,
to the motionless night sky whose patterns negate time
    (those stars, so distant one from the other despite
    appearances)
to the pink dust of every evening.

ۮ

Thinking again of Greece: How could anyone find it surprising that Antigone's farewell to the light is so heartrending and that loved ones in Greek poetry are called 'light of my eyes'? Nowhere have I seen such clarity, so close to crystal but without the least hint of coldness.

ۮ

In the desert, in true disintegration, I still sometimes hear a more or less distant voice talking to me again as I have long been accustomed to hearing poetry speaking to me; in Jean-Michel Frank's last book, for example (*God Save the Roses!*), the two short poems on the death of his mother with these lines:

> *So close to dark soil*
> *Where the rough ground has become foam;*

Or in Kathleen Raine's *On a Deserted Shore*:

> *A night in a bad inn—*
> *But I would say*
> *Guest in love's house;*
> *And blessed and thrice blest*
> *Who walk on earth's sweet grass,*
> *Bathe in time's stream,*
> *And under green boughs rest—*
> *Too short a stay.*[24]

Is it because these poems recreate a unity that may be a trap but to which you aspire all the more as you feel it disintegrating little by little inside you?

❧

How the yellow, pink or purple leaves released suddenly, one by one, at almost regular intervals, falling silently and serenely, magnify the light. We are not capable of this.

≋

Pink and yellow days, days of gentle fire, of silence—
again and again, like an eternal autumn. The colour of
crushed flint.

≋

Cheminements (Wanderings), Jacques Masui's notes,
edited after his death by Pierre-Albert Jourdan.

In our time, there is no room left even for a cry of revolt.
Who would hear it, aside from a few? It is almost no longer
possible to talk to men. That time is past. We must resolve
to keep silent but not give up. *We must follow the move-*
ment within us that leads us forward. The flickering light
that illuminates us must remain lit. The wonder of being
cannot be taken from us, we must rejoice in it until our very
last breath (14 July 1960).

Our age must lead us to total negation . . . but by
causing us to collide with what seems to be absurd . . . it will
offer a few of us, within supreme denial, a last chance to
find the way to the promised land, the land of true seeing.
(20 November 1960)

When, one day, a truly sacred geography has been
established, perhaps then we will learn why certain meadows,
certain valleys, certain cliffs we can remember—having seen
them previously in actuality or in a dream—are pregnant
with a message we experience fully but are unable to express,
much less define (May 1961).

These fragments clearly align with what is best, what is least dubious in me. The last could serve as an epigraph to almost all of my 'landscapes'. But what is missing is all that threatens or harms them.

❧

On waking, the snow running over the road, swept along by a sudden strong wind.

The eight o'clock light in the kitchen, shining on the blue-and-white checkered waxed tablecloth, the snow's reflection. Gather an armful, shiver with cold and with happiness.

❧

It's barely morning, there is barely any light on the kitchen table, barely any disintegration of dawn and the night's cold—just as we ourselves have barely come back to life. There is a profound joy hidden within this meagre dawn, in this break of day that is, more than anything, a reflection of the snow, darkness' slow and silent retreat. The day's bread. Are we thus born once again? Have we landed again?

1979

January

A very beautiful story by Adalbert Stifter, *The Bachelors*.
As in his *Indian Summer*, these pages seem to be illumi-
nated by a sun that is real and familiar, yet supernatural
as well.

ॐ

Schubert's posthumous sonatas are similar: a language
that is at once very near and infinitely far, a web of voices
on different and constantly changing levels, a vein of
melancholy in the most crystalline air.

February

On the radio this morning, an astronomer was explaining
that the farther our observation extends into space, the
more it *moves backwards in time*, with the result that the
discoveries our instruments make millions of light years
away can be considered 'close to the origin'. I had
always been struck by the fact that many of the stars we
see are dead stars, even though they are just as bright
as the others. In this statement, you see the celestial
abyss turn into the abyss of time. Therefore, a sensitive
enough instrument could discern today events on an
inhabited planet that occurred thousands (or millions?)
of years ago. If we applied this principle to the 'near'
world, you would have to say that the moon you are
looking at right now through a telescope is, in fact, the
moon of *x* seconds, minutes or hours ago. This would
even be true, imperceptibly, for what occurs on the earth.
But there, the difference doesn't count. Conversely, it
would be enough to be *today* far enough away from our
planet to be able to see, *today*, Christ's crucifixion, the
Battle of Salamis or Christopher Columbus setting sail
for India.

April

Shells brought back from Forte dei Marmi, the colour of dawn: the birth of Venus.

Ꮷ

Dream. I hear that a Swiss professor is bringing the dead back to life—in the shape of wooden planks that look like playing cards. I see them in a completely Swiss environment of tidy little houses and yards. In order to learn more, we listen to *tomorrow*'s news. In a very foreign-sounding language (Hungarian?), the newsreader announces that the 'Swiss dwarf' is making his own versions. This holds an obscure, monstrous threat. And, in fact, I see through the window two children on their way home from school, followed by their mother (or maid) on a paved path with steep cement banks on either side topped with grassy terraces. The boy has a wooden plaque stuck to his forehead, signifying torment or death.

Ꮷ

Quince trees in bloom behind the Granier farm. Four of five trees in a row of decreasing height (probably because of the wind). Will I one day discern, will I be able to describe their particular beauty, not the beauty of just any flowering fruit tree but one that I find greater than any other?

May

The enclosure at the entrance to the 'wells': an elongated grassy area along the edge of an unseen stream stretching between two bushy hedges and divided by two rows of yellow holm oaks; a world of greens, from light to dark—and within it, the song of nightingales—triple liquidity (of the song, the stream and the burgeoning leaves). It seems out of this world, lost, but marvellously so, and preserved. A reserve. Simple but, as Plotinus says: 'How can one speak about the absolutely simple?'

❧

The large, swollen roses in the warm air, of a colour that almost brings you to tears. Swifts shoot past, the foliage expands. The chestnut flowers observed from up close: strange, almost oriental, like insects pinned into pyramids, brilliant white and pink.

Schubert's Impromptus played by Schnabel. The sound, his breathing, the lines he draws in the interior space like a model. Is what you've been granted a glimpse of a mirage? No, because it is there. It is the draft of the temple drawn by Hölderlin in old age, the internal architectural model, the sonorous rose that blooms on each hearing.

A long, green grass snake, motionless in the branches, watches us with his miniscule head.

Farther off, there are more enclosed spaces, wild. A large wall of yellow stone, covered with ivy and sunlight. Past it, you can see the crowns of small oaks and the light blue sky. Seeing this brings happiness, the sun on the yellow stone and the 'garden' one can make out behind it—with irises and traces of the care someone once took of this now neglected place. And the graceful arch of white-pink dog rose in front of this wall. Stones bound by the gleaming ivy, young and vigorous, calmly growing over them.

On the edge of the path, birthwort grows with its yellowish cones, a flower more bizarre than beautiful, almost wan.

The word 'joy'. Take the time to think about this word. I'm surprised that it suddenly comes back to me.

The dog rose barely supported by its bent and tangled stems, its gentle candour.

June

The full moon, an old companion as mossy as the rocks from which I gaze at it.

The sage on the edge of the path reminds me of the opening of Roud's great prose text which has long sung in my memory: 'flowers on the talus deprived of dew, a pitiful sight for the traveller . . .'

Jourdan's beautiful *Fragments*.

৵

Buffon on the robin redbreast: 'No bird is an earlier riser than this one . . . not very defiant . . . "the woodsman's companion" . . .' Of the nightingale, Buffon wrote that it sings while dreaming during the day. 'The nightingales hide in the densest bushes.'

৵

Descending towards La Tuilière and the Lez, the high, pale green grasses of a truffle field reminded me of Majorca with its olive groves overgrown with grass or wheat. The word 'Parnassus' came to mind. Then, past a half-circle of very tall and noble oak trees—wheat still a very pale shade of yellow, the grass, the silvery trees

on the riverside where there is almost no more water. A
mulberry tree, half split by the wind, creaks like a door.

જ⁊

The oriole, bright yellow and black, glimpsed in the oak
grove that lines the road.

Timothy-grass, festucas, bromus . . .

A very large yellow and black ladybird hangs in an
oak tree, as immobile as a totem. Even when very near,
the nightingales remain invisible.

જ⁊

A dream I remember rather well for having been torn
from it by one of our neighbour's coughing fits, which
we always worry might be his death throes.

It was, essentially, a series of 'views', each of which
seemed to me, as a traveller, more beautiful, more sur-
prising, mysterious and exhilarating than the last. There
was the sea, a distant chain of mountains and a city I
associated (at least now and then) with Lisbon. I believe
I began by admiring the facade of a palace someone was
showing me. On the facade, there was a row of standing
figures or at least of expressive faces, the colour of earth,
in the style of elaborately Baroque pilasters. Then this
changed into a series of busts also lined side by side on
some kind of shelving in a room. Women's scarves were
tied across the faces of some (three?) of the busts, more

or less like veils. The man next to me explained that this was the local custom and that he was going to look for something to veil another one. (Later in this dream, I notice that a long range of hills has also been veiled in this manner.) It's perhaps the same man who then tells me he is heading to China (or Chile?) behind these mountains, past this mountain range.

Nevertheless, I was glad to get back to Lisbon (although the city bore no real resemblance to it). For a moment, between two window mullions or two close-set walls, I glimpsed a small group of houses in the distance, also in dark earth tones. One of them had a barrel vault facade like a carriage gate. It was all so beautiful, I exclaimed to my friend J. E., 'A piece of Italy!' He answered, 'African, rather.' And, indeed, there was a palm tree behind the houses, perhaps. But the essential part of the dream is that these views evoked in me such profound admiration, exaltation even, that I was close to tears.

Some travelling companions appeared, a Swiss couple with two children. I think their name was Ziegler. Madame Ziegler's erudite commentary, citing dates like the twelfth and thirteenth centuries, annoyed me (because I knew less than she and because my emotions seemed to be of a different order), and I wanted to go off and enjoy the beauty of the sights alone. So I went into the house and found François J. in a large room. He had turned into the twelve-year-old boy he was when I first met him. There was another child with him. They were writing a letter of condolence to my aunt M. for her husband's death (both had been dead for years but I had recently learnt that their oldest son, to whom I was closer than to most of my other cousins, was ill). François asked me how he should address my aunt, having come up with phrases that were touching, tender and rather extravagant (and both boys were leafing through an old family picture album to find illustrations for their letter). I remember telling him that in the circumstances, he shouldn't get too imaginative but still maintain a certain freshness. He could write, for example, 'My most amiable Aunt M.', or something similar. Then I realized that I too should write to her and in my letter I told her about the uncle who must have visited Lisbon on one of his many voyages.

Later, somewhere else, in a garden in front of a house with a modest, classical pediment covered with wisteria, I found a well with three statues of that same shade of ochre. And once again, the beauty of this place was profound and indescribable. Approaching the well, I saw that one of the statues looked like Julius Caesar and that each of them could spin on its axis (or all three revolve round the well). And then, as if to prevent me from contemplating all these wonders, a voice called me.

At one point, someone, a bartender, perhaps, showed me a block of stone like those from which the town was built, and pointed out that it wasn't solid. Thinking of the Hieronymites Monastery (Lisbon, still), I answered that this doesn't prevent the city from being beautiful.

This last comment seems to be a delayed answer to an Englishwoman I had spoken to earlier that night at my friends' house. She had told me that she admired the style of my writing, but did not appreciate the subject matter or could not understand it (that approach to nature, with which they, the English, have a much more 'natural' rapport).

Should I associate the bandaged busts and hills in my dream with the fact that I had cut myself slightly at dinner and had to dress the wound? Then extend it to symbols of castration? Such explanations, however valid for different levels of lived experiences, would not come close to addressing the mysterious beauty of the 'views' and the joy they filled me with, one after the other.

July

A full moon emerges from the leaves like a rose; crossed, escorted by rapidly flying swifts black as coal. Heat.

ॐ

Large fields of wheat and oat under a blue-grey sky, framed by oaks. The sound of straw from the wind in the ears of wheat.

Willows at the pond, shadows move among their silvery leaves, shadows tied to their leaves, as if internal: the metamorphosis of a water nymph, a liquid Daphnis. Not a single cloud. The power of the pale wheat, lavender alive with butterflies.

ॐ

Stardust, cloud of the Milky Way. Close your eyes. The sound of crickets, like little sleigh bells or rather like the ringing of dried grass in the meadow. Pale colours, pink, straw yellow, grey, blue, mauve.

August

A Purcell concert in the Church of Saint-Florent in Orange. The shadow of the neoclassical altar on the stone wall (two Corinthian columns, a canopy topped with a kind of panache) forms the perfect backdrop to the incidental music in *Dido and Aeneas*, like the ports in paintings by Claude Lorrain. You would not be surprised to see the shadow of suffering Dido rise between these columns.

໕

This morning, despite the heat, the very first sign of autumn appeared, a shred of fog far off in the folds of the hills and the fields. The warbler, with its resonant song, is still here, between the acacia and the linden trees. Orpheus in the summer garden. You can say that it too passes easily from one realm into another. Would I ever have been able to follow it?

NOTES

1 Simone Weil, *Attente de Dieu: Lettres, 1942* (Waiting for God: Letters, 1942) (Paris: Editions Fayard, 1966), pp. 92f. This and other translations of quoted material are mine, unless mentioned otherwise. [Trans.]

2 E. M. Cioran, *History and Utopia* (Richard Howard trans.) (London: Quartet Books, 1987), p. 118.

3 Meister Eckhart, *Selected Writings* (Oliver Davies trans.) (London: Penguin, 1995), pp. 233f.

4 Luis de Góngora, *The Solitudes* (Edith Grossman trans.) (New York: Penguin, 2011), pp. 73, 81.

5 R. H. Blyth, *Haiku*, VOLS 1–4 (Tokyo: Hokuseido, 1951–52).

6 Blyth, *Haiku*, VOL. 2, p. 55.

7 Jacques Dupin, *Fits and Starts* (Paul Auster trans.) (Berkeley, CA: Living Hand, 1973), p. 14.

8 Jules Superveille, *Le forçat innocent* (The Innocent Convict) (Paris: Gallimard, 1969), p. 258.

9 Blyth, *Haiku*, VOL. 2, p. 196.

10 Ibid., p. 312.

11 Ibid., p. 371.

12 Ibid., VOL. 3, p. 72.

13 Jorge Luis Borges, *Selected Nonfiction* (Eliot Weinberger ed. and trans.) (London: Penguin, 2000), p. 54.

14 Plato, *The Dialogues of Plato, Translated into English with Analyses and Introductions by B. Jowett, M.A. in Five Volumes*, VOL. 1 (Oxford: Clarendon, 1892), p. 466.

15 'I believe only the histories, whose witnesses got themselves killed.' Blaise Pascal, *Thoughts* (W. F. Trotter trans.), VOL. 48, PART 1 of *The Harvard Classics* (New York: P. F. Collier, 1909–14), NO. 593.

16 Plotinus, *The Enneads* (Stephen MacKenna trans.) (London: Penguin, 1991), p. 32.

17 Ibid., p. 127.

18 Ibid., p. 143.

19 Léon Chestov, *Le Pouvoir des Clefs* (Potestas Clavium) (Boris de Schloezer trans.) (Paris: Flammarion, 1967).

20 Georges Bataille, *Erotism: Death and Sensuality* (Mary Dalwood trans.) (San Francisco: City Lights, 1986), p. 40.

21 Ibid., p. 91.

22 Alexander Pushkin, *The Little Tragedies* (Nancy Anderson trans.) (New Haven, CT: Yale University Press, 2000), pp. 101f.

23 Friedrich Nietzsche, 'Miscellaneous Maxims and Opinions, no. 183' in *Human, All-Too-Human, Part II: A Book for Free Spirits* (Paul V. Cohn trans.) (New York: Macmillan, 1913), p. 98.

24 Kathleen Raine, *On a Deserted Shore* (London: Dolmen, 1973), NO. 44.